RAPE CULTURE

HOW CAN WE END IT?

By Michelle Denton

LUCENT
PRESS

Published in 2018 by
Lucent Press, an Imprint of Greenhaven Publishing, LLC
353 3rd Avenue
Suite 255
New York, NY 10010

Designer: Seth Hughes
Editor: Jennifer Lombardo

Library of Congress Cataloging-in-Publication Data

Names: Denton, Michelle, author.
Title: Rape culture : how can we end it? / Michelle Denton.
Description: New York : Lucent Press, [2018] | Series: Hot topics | Includes
    bibliographical references and index.
Identifiers: LCCN 2017051347| ISBN 9781534562073 (library bound book) | ISBN
    9781534562929 (pbk. book) | ISBN9781534562080 (ebook)
Subjects: LCSH: Rape–United States–Juvenile literature. | Sex
    crimes–United States–Juvenile literature. | Sexual abuse victims–United
    States–Juvenile literature. | Sexual ethics–United States–Juvenile
    literature.
Classification: LCC HV6561 .D46 2018 | DDC 364.15/320973–dc23
LC record available at https://lccn.loc.gov/2017051347

Printed in the United States of America

CPSIA compliance information: Batch #CW18KL: For further information contact Greenhaven Publishing LLC, New York,
New York at 1-844-317-7404.

CONTENTS

Adolescence is a time when many people begin to take notice of the world around them. News channels, blogs, and talk radio shows are constantly promoting one view or another; very few are unbiased. Young people also hear conflicting information from parents, friends, teachers, and acquaintances. Often, they will hear only one side of an issue or be given flawed information. People who are trying to support a particular viewpoint may cite inaccurate facts and statistics on their blogs, and news programs present many conflicting views of important issues in our society. In a world where it seems everyone has a platform to share their thoughts, it can be difficult to find unbiased, accurate information about important issues.

It is not only facts that are important. In blog posts, in comments on online videos, and on talk shows, people will share opinions that are not necessarily true or false, but can still have a strong impact. For example, many young people struggle with their body image. Seeing or hearing negative comments about particular body types online can have a huge effect on the way someone views himself or herself and may lead to depression and anxiety. Although it is important not to keep information hidden from young people under the guise of protecting them, it is equally important to offer encouragement on issues that affect their mental health.

The titles in the Hot Topics series provide readers with different viewpoints on important issues in today's society. Many of these issues, such as teen pregnancy and Internet safety, are of immediate concern to young people. This series aims to give readers factual context on these crucial topics in a way that lets them form their own opinions. The facts presented throughout also serve to empower readers to help themselves or support people they know who are struggling with many of the challenges adolescents face today. Although negative viewpoints are not ignored or downplayed, this series allows young people to see that the challenges they face are not insurmountable. Eating disorders can be overcome, the Internet can be navigated safely, and pregnant teens do not have to feel hopeless.

Quotes encompassing all viewpoints are presented and cited so readers can trace them back to their original source, verifying for themselves whether the information comes from a reputable place. Additional books and websites are listed, giving readers a starting point from which to continue their own research. Chapter questions encourage discussion, allowing young people to hear and understand their classmates' points of view as they further solidify their own. Full-color photographs and enlightening charts provide a deeper understanding of the topics at hand. All of these features augment the informative text, helping young people understand the world they live in and formulate their own opinions concerning the best way they can improve it.

A Serious Violation

Ashley had it all: a 4.0 GPA, the lead role in the school play, and a new spot as drum major for her school's marching band. At 13, the most stressful thing in her life was waiting for an acceptance letter from one of the best high schools in the state. That, however, changed quickly because of a boy named Steven. Steven, someone Ashley considered a friend, pressured her into playing strip poker after school one day and later demanded oral sex. This happened three times, and each time, Ashley felt too scared to say no. "I felt violated," she wrote in a 2016 open letter. "I felt like a slut. He occasionally passed me a note or wrote me a letter saying I was a whore, a slut, and that I was no good. I didn't report it for fear he would turn the story around."[1] Although she eventually found support among real friends, Ashley never reported this to the authorities, and the good things in her life became overshadowed by feelings of fear and guilt.

Unfortunately, Ashley's story is a common one. Two out of every three instances of sexual violence go unreported, and there are over 321,000 victims of rape and sexual assault every year in the United States. In a study done over the course of five years, rape survivors cited many reasons why they decided not to report the crime. Some feared revenge from the perpetrator, some believed the police could not or would not help, and some simply thought it was not important enough to involve the authorities. Reasons like these come from a long history of rape not being taken seriously. People joke about rape and often say that those who come forward as rape victims deserved it or are lying about it for attention. Additionally, the U.S. criminal justice system regularly drops sexual assault cases due to insufficient evidence and attempts to protect the reputations of sexual predators. Rape culture, where dismissing the victim and defending the criminal is the norm, only empowers people who harm others for their own benefit, and it needs to be stopped.

Sexual assault can make victims feel depressed and isolated, making it difficult for them to find help.

Forms and Definitions

Sexual violence comes in many different forms. In the United States, rape is legally defined as "penetration, no matter how slight, of the vagina or anus with any body part or object, or oral penetration by a sex organ of another person, without the consent of the victim,"[2] but sexual assault does not always involve rape. Sexual assault also includes attempted rape, unwanted sexual touching, and forced participation in any sexual act, and these acts are equally as illegal as nonconsensual penetration. Even sexual harassment—which, according to the Equal Employment Opportunity Commission, involves "unwelcome sexual advances, requests for sexual favors, and other verbal or physical harassment of a sexual nature"[3]—is considered criminal.

Explaining Consent with Tea

Because some people have a difficult time understanding consent, people have attempted to explain it in simpler terms. One video that has been widely viewed involves comparing offering sex to offering a cup of tea. In this metaphor, if a person asks their friend if they would like a cup of tea and they enthusiastically say they would love one, then it is easy to tell they want the tea. If they say they are unsure, "then you could make them a cup of tea (or not), but be aware they might not drink it. And if they don't drink it, then—and this is the important part—don't make them drink it. Just because you made it doesn't mean you are entitled to watch them drink it."[1] If the person says they definitely do not want tea, their friend should not make them tea, force them to drink tea, or be offended that they refused the cup of tea.

The video also discusses an important part of consent—someone's ability to change their mind: "They might say, 'Yes please, that's kind of you.' And then when the tea arrives, they actually don't want the tea at all. Sure, that's kind of annoying, as you've gone to all the effort of making the tea, but they remain under no obligation to drink the tea."[2] Other situations involving consent are also discussed in the video, which can be viewed on YouTube. Some people have criticized the video, saying that it oversimplifies the issue and that people do not view guilting someone into drinking tea the same way they view guilting someone into having sex. Others have praised it, saying that it gives a good overview of consent in simple terms everyone can understand.

1. "Tea Consent," YouTube video, 2:50, posted by Blue Seat Studios, May 12, 2015. www.youtube.com/watch?v=oQbei5JGiT8.
2. "Tea Consent," YouTube video, posted by Blue Seat Studios.

"Consent" is the most important word to remember when thinking about the forms of sexual violence. Giving consent means agreeing, so any sexual act committed without both people agreeing to it is assault. In some cases, this means that one person actively says no, and in other cases, this means that one person is unable to say no because of mental illness or disability, unconsciousness, or intoxication, or because they are being lied to. Age is also a factor because someone under the age of consent—generally 16 or 18 depending on the state or country—cannot legally give consent to anyone. Even if a person says yes to a sexual act, they may be the victim of a sex crime if they have been emotionally or psychologically manipulated. Sexual predators often threaten or guilt their targets into saying yes, which is called coercion. Under all circumstances, anything less than enthusiastic, willing consent to something sexual is considered a "no."

Defining Rape Culture

Culture is considered everything a group of people thinks and does. Beliefs, values, traditions, art, religion, social behavior—all of these things and more express a society's culture and at the same time create it. Every new idea or action becomes part of a group's history and influences its future, making culture an ever-evolving system. This is why no time period looks exactly like the one before it. However, people often do not see this; they believe that the way things in their society are during their lifetime is the way things will be or should be forever. Because of this belief, elements of culture, such as a certain value or behavior, are passed down from one generation to the next on an individual basis, generally from parent to child. If enough individuals pass on the same element, it remains a part of the culture until the next generation decides whether or not to pass it down again.

Unfortunately, harmful elements of culture are passed down just as easily as useful ones. The normalization of sexual violence, for example, has been taught to every generation of humans so far. This is what feminists in the 1970s called "rape culture," a culture in which sexual assault is an expected, seemingly inevitable part of life, particularly for women. The reality is that one out of every six women will be the victim of an attempted or completed rape, and one out of every four or five will experience sexual assault. (Statistics vary because so many instances go

Generation after generation passes down their culture and knowledge to future generations, but unlike a love of reading, not every tradition that gets passed down is necessarily good.

unreported.) However, those numbers would plummet if Western culture did not encourage male aggression and the objectification of women. If rapists did not believe they could get away with rape, they would be less likely to do it. If they did not see women as objects, they would be less likely to use them as such. If they did not believe "no means yes," they would be less likely to ignore a "no" when they heard it. If they did not believe a "real" man must be aggressive, they would be less likely to use rape to make themselves feel more powerful.

Change can happen. With every generation comes a new opportunity to erase destructive parts of a culture by teaching children better ways of thinking. Undoing rape culture will not happen overnight, but examining its causes and effects and working to fix them will go a long way toward making the world a safer, happier place.

Cultural Roots

Even though culture is always evolving, most modern cultures still have elements handed down from ancient ones. Western culture—the culture found in Europe, North America, Australia, and their colonies and territories—is mainly the product of ancient Greece and Rome, as well as early Christian societies. In general, Western civilization places importance on freedom of thought, human rights, and democracy, although these values vary among countries.

While the cultural legacies of these ancient societies continue to inspire art, music, and literature today, the modern world has also adopted some of their worst problems. Although most people like to think that Western culture is enlightened and fair, the mistreatment of women during the early days of Western civilization has only evolved, much like the rest of the culture, and it continues to harm the whole society. The origins of rape culture lie in the ancient past, in old ways of thinking, and in unresolved struggles for equality.

Property Damage in Ancient Rome

In ancient Rome, women were considered the property and responsibility of their paterfamilias, the male head of the household they lived in. Ownership of a woman passed from her father (or oldest brother, if her father had died) to her husband the day she married. It was not until late Roman history that women were given individual names. Lawyer Nghiem L. Nguyen explained:

> For instance, names such as Julia, Claudia, and Cornelia were simply family names with feminine endings attached, and often daughters within one family had the same name and were distinguished only by the addition of "elder" or "younger." This system of naming suggests the desire to identify women as merely passive units within a family, and not as genuine, independent individuals.[4]

Freeborn Roman women were seen as a commodity, not much different than slaves. A woman's purpose, the Romans believed, was to have children and continue their husband's family's lineage. Because they served only this one purpose, their sexual purity was of the utmost importance. A woman who had intercourse before she was married or with anyone besides her husband after she was married was considered damaged goods, even if it was against her will. "Instead of being seen as victims," Nguyen said, "raped women were seen as sources of embarrassment to their husbands and fathers. With the loss of their virginity, unmarried women had little hope for a marriage, and married victims suffered shame and despair."[5] In the aftermath of a rape, some victims were even killed to remove the perceived weakness from their families in the eyes of the community. While the rapist also generally faced consequences, they were rarely so severe and often only amounted to repaying the family as if he had broken a statue.

Roman women were treated like pottery—useful until they were "damaged."

While the consequences for convicted rapists are much harsher now than they were during the Roman Empire, rape survivors sometimes face similar social disgrace. Sexual purity is still considered significant in today's society, especially in religious circles, so women often feel dirty or tainted after being sexually assaulted. Some romantic partners view rape as cheating and leave victims for being unfaithful. Although rape does not define a person and does not reflect on their character, being exposed to society's beliefs about rape can cause shame and guilt even though the victim is never at fault.

A Made-Up Concept

Although ancient and modern cultures put a great deal of emphasis on virginity, people are beginning to see the idea of sexual purity for what it really is: a social construct. In sociology—the scientific study of society and social interaction—a social construct is an idea about reality that a culture has accepted. Not all of them are bad, but many are nothing more than restrictions. In the case of virginity, Anne Thériault of *Thought Catalog* said, "It is a way of policing other people's bodies and passing judgment on how they use them. It is, at its very core, a way of controlling and subjugating women."[1]

Western culture has long believed that there is something about having sex for the first time that fundamentally changes a person. For centuries, women were told only two things about sex. The first was that they should only have it with their husband, and the second, told to them on the day of their wedding, was that it was going to hurt. Women were expected to bleed due to the tearing of the hymen, a thin membrane that partially closes the vagina. If a woman did not bleed on her wedding night, she was shunned, and it could be grounds for divorce because she was assumed to have lost her virginity to someone other than her husband. Today, it is commonly known that not all women are born with a hymen, and there are lots of ways it could be torn other than penetrative sex. More importantly, medical experts now know that a woman does not ever need to be in pain during sex, even during her first time.

1. Anne Thériault, "Virginity Is a Social Construct," *Thought Catalog*, April 10, 2014. thoughtcatalog.com/anne-theriault/2014/04/virginity-is-a-social-construct/.

Myths and Legends

Myths, or stories dealing with "the human condition, good and evil, human origins, life and death, the afterlife, and the gods,"[6] are found in every culture, both modern and ancient. To historians and anthropologists studying ancient cultures, mythology serves as a window into the beliefs and values held thousands of years ago. However, in studying ancient Greece and Rome, disturbing ideas about sexual assault come to light.

In Greek mythology, Zeus, king of the gods, is famous for seducing many mortal women. Consent, however, was a foreign concept, and some of these encounters were against the woman's will. Among these women assaulted was Leda, queen of Sparta, for whom Zeus turned himself into a swan. In some versions of the myth, Leda is seduced by Zeus and consents to sex with him, but in other versions, it is implied that Zeus rapes her. Although it is difficult now to determine which version is the one ancient Greeks were telling, the fact that the rape version exists at all says a great deal. If Leda was raped by Zeus, the Greeks overlooked it because she became pregnant with Helen, the woman who was blamed for the Trojan War, as well as Castor and Pollux, the twins that make up the Gemini constellation. In this and many other cases in Greek mythology, the rape was excused because the victim became pregnant with important legendary figures.

In line with Roman ideas about rape is their interpretation of the Greek myth of Medusa, a Gorgon—a monster with snakes for hair who turned anyone who looked at her to stone. Ovid, a Roman writer, wrote that Medusa had once been a beautiful human, but she was cursed by Minerva, the goddess of wisdom, after being raped in her temple by Neptune, the god of the ocean. Ovid's story makes Medusa's hideousness a punishment for being sexually assaulted, reinforcing Roman society's belief that the victim, not the rapist, should be punished more severely.

Rape is even found as an important reason for Rome's early success. A mixture of history and legend, the story goes that Rome was founded sometime around 750 BC by Romulus, but although the city grew very quickly, there was a shortage of women. Romulus worried that his new city would crumble since there were not enough women to create a second generation of Romans, and none of the surrounding cities were willing to form an alliance. To secure his legacy, Romulus invited Rome's neighbors, the Sabines, to a festival, and when the entire tribe had arrived, the Romans stole the Sabine women and killed all the men. It is hard to imagine that the Sabine women would have consented to becoming the mothers of Rome when every man there had killed their husbands, sons, and fathers, so they were most likely forced. In this story, a foundational tale of the history of Rome, the rape of the Sabine women is supposedly justified because it was necessary for the city to remain strong and continue on, and the women eventually accept this view. To ancient Romans who heard this story, the future of the city was more important than the Sabine women's suffering. This story inspired several famous paintings, proving that later generations viewed the women's suffering as important and inspirational.

The Rape of the Sabine Women *by Nicolas Poussin is one of many works of art based on the incident between the Romans and the Sabines. The story inspired artists throughout the Renaissance and post-Renaissance eras.*

Rape as part of a divine plan is a topic of heated debate in today's world. While it is generally not looked at as a punishment anymore, like in Medusa's story, it is still sometimes considered a good thing when the rape victim becomes pregnant. In the United States, conservative Christian groups and politicians oppose abortion by arguing that every child is created by the will of God, even those conceived during a rape. Because carrying the child of their rapist could be psychologically scarring, women are currently able to terminate their pregnancy in these situations, but some people believe it should be illegal to have an abortion even if the woman was raped. Like Leda and the Sabine women, the emotional and physical suffering of modern rape survivors is made secondary to the perceived importance of their pregnancy.

Inside and Outside the City Walls

In ancient Israel, the Hebrew Bible was looked to for guidance through most parts of daily life, including the law. The first five books of the Bible—known as the Mosaic Law, the Torah, or the Pentateuch—gave the laws of the land, including extremely specific instructions about what to do with rapists and their victims. Primarily, these laws applied to unmarried women since their virginity was highly prized.

In Deuteronomy chapter 22, the Mosaic Law says that if an engaged woman is discovered to have been raped inside the city, both she and her rapist should be put to death. In these cases, it continues, her rape should have been avoidable since someone in the city would have heard her scream. Since she was not heard screaming, the sex must have been consensual, making it adultery—sex with someone other than one's spouse—instead of rape. Adultery was punishable by death, and an engaged woman was considered already married even though she had not slept with her husband or moved into his house yet. However, the law goes on to say that if an engaged woman is discovered to have been raped outside the city walls—in the field—only her rapist should be put to death. This is because no one could have heard her scream.

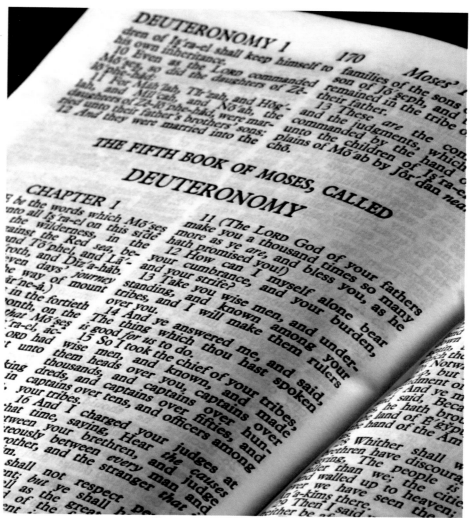

The Book of Deuteronomy is one of the first five books of the Bible, which is called the Torah or the Pentateuch. These books contain the Mosaic Law—rules Moses expected the Israelites to follow in Canaan, the "promised land."

Deuteronomy 22 continues,

If a man meets a virgin who is not betrothed [engaged], and seizes her and lies with her, and they are found, then the man who lay with her shall give to the father of the young woman fifty shekels of silver, and she shall be his wife, because he has violated her; he may not put her away [divorce her] all his days.[7]

It is likely that this law came about because a rape victim was considered unclean. No one would ever marry her, robbing her family of the money her husband would pay them for her, so the rapist was expected to take the burden of marrying her as punishment. Although the young woman was seen as a victim, that did not change the fact that she had lost her worth. Instead of being put to death, she was forced to marry her attacker, a situation some considered to be worse.

Putting the responsibility of not being raped on the victim remains a common problem in modern discussions about preventing sexual assault. Today, women are told to learn self-defense, to not drink alcohol at parties, to wear more clothing, to stop taking public transportation, and many other things to reduce their risk of being raped. A college in Colorado went so far as to suggest that women urinate or vomit if they are attacked as a way to disgust their attacker and possibly prevent the assault from continuing. These suggestions range from practical to ridiculous, but none target the real issue: It is not a woman's responsibility to not be raped. It is society's responsibility to teach people not to rape in the first place.

False Accusations

A commonly held belief about rape victims is that most of them are lying. This belief seems to survive no matter how many times it is proven to be false. Throughout history and up until today, rape victims who come forward about their attack are often assumed to be lying for attention or trying to ruin the accused man's life in an act of revenge. While it would be false to say that this has never happened—between 2 percent and 10 percent of rape allegations are proven to be false—it is unfair and cruel to assume a victim of sexual assault is lying. In Western culture, two ancient stories were the basis of this idea: the Greek story of Phaedra, queen of Athens, and the biblical story of Potiphar's unnamed wife.

Ancient Greek mythology was generally only written down in the form of plays or epic poetry, combining art, religion, and history into one. Euripides, one of the most famous ancient Greek playwrights, wrote the play *Hippolytus* around 428 BC, dramatizing the story of Hippolytus, son of Theseus—the king of Athens—and the revenge against Hippolytus by Aphrodite, the goddess of love. In the play, Hippolytus refuses to worship Aphrodite, so she makes his stepmother, Phaedra, fall in love with him. After her affections are rejected, Phaedra hangs herself, leaving a note saying that Hippolytus had raped her. In a rage, Theseus curses his son to be killed by sea monsters, and Hippolytus's innocence is proven by the goddess Artemis too late to save him from his father's curse. Although she is forced to love her stepson by Aphrodite's magic, Phaedra is made out to be the villain of the play. She accuses Hippolytus of rape so he will not be able to tell his father that she loved him, covering up her own guilt by making Hippolytus seem guilty of something far worse.

In Pierre Narcisse Guerin's Phaedra and Hippolytus, *Hippolytus rejects his stepmother, leading to his doom.*

A similar story appears in the Bible. One of the main heroes in Genesis, the first book of the Bible, is Joseph, the best-loved son of Jacob. At the beginning of his story, he is sold into slavery by his brothers and bought by an Egyptian named Potiphar, a high-ranking official under the pharaoh. Joseph is quick to earn his master's respect and is made overseer of Potiphar's house and fields, but he also catches the eye of Potiphar's wife. She attempts to seduce him several times, but each time he refuses. After being rejected again and again, Potiphar's wife accuses Joseph of raping her and has him thrown in prison.

IMPROVING RESPONSE

"Research shows that rates of false reporting are frequently inflated, in part because of inconsistent definitions and protocols, or a weak understanding of sexual assault. Misconceptions about false reporting rates have direct, negative consequences and can contribute to why many victims don't report sexual assaults. To improve the response to victims of sexual violence, law enforcement and service providers need a thorough understanding of sexual violence and consistency in their definitions, policies and procedures."

−report from the National Sexual Violence Resource Center

"False Reporting," National Sexual Violence Resource Center, 2012. www.nsvrc.org/sites/default/files/Publications_NSVRC_Overview_False-Reporting.pdf.

Although Joseph does not die like Hippolytus does, both men are the innocent victims of lustful women. Since the Bible and Greek mythology shape so much of Western culture, these stories of a woman falsely accusing a man of rape as revenge are often misused to represent all women who accuse men of rape. The question of how to deal with the reality of false rape accusations is one that sparks heated debate. Western society cannot ignore the most basic rule of the legal system—that everyone is innocent until proven guilty—but it also cannot ignore the vital need for rape victims to be believed when they come forward. Donna Zuckerberg, editor of *Eidolon*, an online Classics journal, wrote:

If we believe that alleged rapists are innocent until proven guilty, then on some level, we have to believe that victims might be lying until they can prove that they're telling the truth. We don't want to automatically assume that everyone accused is a rapist, but we also don't want to assume that accusers are liars. There is no unequivocally safe ground from which to judge.[8]

The gray area surrounding rape accusations makes many people uncomfortable, but the conversation needs to continue in order to break through the discomfort and come to an understanding about the way rape victims should be treated in the future.

Victim-Blaming in Medieval England

The medieval period, or Middle Ages, in England is considered to have lasted from AD 1154 to 1485, and it was a brutal time to be alive. Disease, starvation, and poverty were constant worries for the average person, and with the Christian church at the center of daily life, so was damnation. In a culture controlled by church teachings, sin was the ultimate crime, and everything from murder to petty theft was punished with either serious mutilation or public execution. Justice was served swiftly and with very little public outcry against it.

However, men accused of rape were often let go. Rape became a felony in England in 1285, but it was rare for these cases to end in punishment. "In the English Midlands between 1400 and 1430," said historian Sean McGlynn, "of 280 rape cases, not one led to a conviction. For the country as a whole in the first three-quarters of the thirteenth century, only one prosecution out of 142 resulted in so much as a fine."[9] The problem lay with Church doctrine; Eve, the first woman according to the Bible, tempted Adam to eat the fruit of knowledge and got them both expelled from Eden, forever framing women in the same way. Medieval women were portrayed as temptresses, one sexual encounter away from becoming demons of lust and dragging men, who were morally superior, into Hell with them. Sexual assault, then, was considered the woman's fault; it was thought that she must have done something to provoke her rapist and therefore deserved to be raped. "Questions of proof of consent, the lack of witnesses, and the reluctance of an all-male jury to pass a death sentence,"[10] as well as calling into question the rape victim's moral character, all made it easy for accused rapists to stay out of prison.

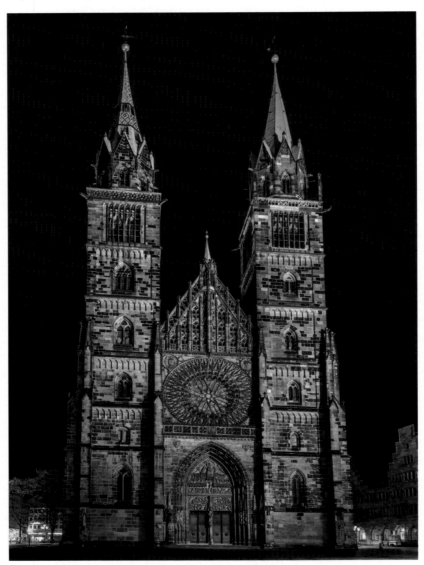

The Christian church ruled over medieval life, sometimes having more power than the king.

The only justice a woman could find was in self-defense. Although a woman harming or killing a man for no reason was condemned as treason because it went against the "natural order," harming or killing a man who was trying to sexually assault her suggested that she truly had not consented. For example, in 1438, a woman named Joan Chapelyn was let off for killing the Frenchman who was raping her. The verdict was rare but not impossible.

In the same way that medieval women were accused of being temptresses, modern women are also likely to be blamed for their sexual assault. From the moment they come forward, rape survivors are looked at critically. The police, the media, and even close friends and family are likely to ask questions such as, "What were you wearing?" or "Were you leading him on?" These kinds of comments are more likely to be directed at heterosexual female or gay male victims who are attacked by men. They are harmful because they put the blame on the victim for somehow tempting their attacker, even though rape can happen regardless of what the person was wearing or what they were doing. Heterosexual men who are victimized by women may be more likely to be asked questions such as, "Were you aroused?" or "Was she hot?" This implies they either wanted or should have wanted to have sex with their attacker. The myth that men always want sex with any woman who shows interest makes many people falsely believe that men cannot be raped, and a male rape victim may be called "lucky," especially by other men. This invalidates the pain and fear that rape causes, no matter what sex the rapist and victim are.

Women also sometimes assault other women, but these stories are almost never talked about, to the point that many people falsely believe it does not happen. Even when this is reported, it is often dismissed by police—just like men who report being raped by a woman—because it is generally assumed that women are not capable of committing that kind of violent act, either because they are too physically weak or they are too morally superior. Women who report an assault by another woman may also encounter the attitude that they are blowing a "girl fight" out of proportion. If they are bisexual or lesbian, they may encounter the same belief heterosexual male rape victims do: that everyone who is interested in women will always want to have sex with one when the opportunity is presented. Even heterosexual women are often dismissed, as they are perceived as being more open to same-sex sexual activity than heterosexual men are. In some states, rape laws specifically include the words "penis" or "opposite sex," meaning a woman who was raped by another woman may not be able to press charges. Even people who take male-on-female sexual violence seriously may not do the same for female-on-male or female-on-female sexual violence.

Adam's First Wife

In some Jewish interpretations of the book of Genesis, Adam had a wife before Eve. Lilith, whose name means "night," fits into Genesis 1, where both man and woman are made from the earth at the same time, unlike Genesis 2, where they are made one after the other and Eve is made from Adam's rib. A ninth- or tenth-century collection of legends called the *Alphabet of Ben Sira* expanded on this interpretation, creating a mythology in which Lilith, who sees herself as equal to Adam, refuses to submit to him, escapes the garden of Eden, and becomes a demon. She becomes a symbol of uncontrolled female sexuality, and in medieval times, people believed she or her children, the succubae, would seduce men in their sleep and cause all sorts of illnesses. Today, Lilith is a feminist hero to women who see her rebellion as a rejection of male domination.

The Era of Hysteria

"Hysteria" was once a medical term describing a mental disorder found only in women that caused "faintness, nervousness, insomnia, fluid retention, heaviness in abdomen, muscle spasm, shortness of breath, irritability, loss of appetite for food or sex, and 'a tendency to cause trouble.'"[11] It was believed to be caused by abnormal movement of the uterus, and since men do not have a uterus, it was considered impossible for them to have hysteria. The concept, in one form or another, has been around since ancient Egypt, but it gained popularity in the 1800s as psychology became the science of the day. It is also entirely fake.

This is not to say that the symptoms were not real. In mild forms, every symptom doctors looked for to diagnose hysteria is a possible effect of premenstrual syndrome, or PMS, which is caused by the fluctuation of hormones that happens before someone begins menstruating every month.

In more extreme cases, women who would have been considered hysterical two centuries ago are now diagnosed with disorders such as schizophrenia, anxiety, post-traumatic stress disorder (PTSD), or conversion, which is when a patient experiences blindness or paralysis with no medical explanation. During the Victorian era, however, doctors had a more limited understanding of the human brain and often described many different mental illnesses with one umbrella term, not making the distinction between them and causing confusion for themselves and the public. It is also important to note that when these disorders arise today, they occur in both men and women. Social stigma has always kept the number of men who seek psychological help low because many societies view asking for help as weak behavior, making it likely that in the Victorian era, the overwhelming majority of patients with these symptoms were women only because men were not reporting it. This, along with the disorder's connection to PMS, created the false perception that "hysteria" was exclusively a woman's disease.

Women were already considered the "weaker sex," prone to fainting when their emotions were high, and both boys and girls were raised to believe that women were burdens on their families because they were so helpless. Just like in ancient times, a woman's only purpose was to have children and take care of the house while her husband worked, and anything outside of that was seen as abnormal. Hysteria became the explanation for almost every "unwomanly" behavior a woman might exhibit, such as being argumentative or, worst of all, refusing to have sex with her husband. Sex was thought of as a husband's right, perhaps as payment for taking on the burden of his so-called helpless wife, so the rate of marital rape was very high. This idea has unfortunately persisted today to the point that many people believe a married person cannot be raped. However, a marriage vow is not automatic consent to sex; consent must be willingly given every time.

Victorian women were already thought to be fragile and highly emotional, and the concept of hysteria only made it worse.

A woman might have been diagnosed with hysteria because she refused to submit to her husband sexually and would have been sent to see a doctor who might also rape her in the name of treatment. Hysteria was believed to be the result of sexual dissatisfaction, so a "pelvic massage" was often used as a cure— "pelvic massage" being the polite term doctors used to describe sexually assaulting their patients.

The idea of a mental disorder that only affected women made discrediting women incredibly easy. If a woman came forward about abuse, sexual or otherwise, she could be said to be imagining it, and if the symptoms became extreme enough, she could be sent to an asylum. In some ways, it was a medical misunderstanding—the doctors did not have an explanation for what was wrong with their patients, so they diagnosed and treated them in the only ways they knew how to—but in other ways, the entire concept of hysteria was also a way for men to justify the way they treated women. If women, and only women, were likely to lose their minds for what seemed like no reason, then they were as helpless as everyone said. Even today, women are discredited because they are seen as more irrationally emotional than men. This kind of thinking props up ideas of women as temptresses and false rape accusers—a view that aids rapists by creating doubt when someone comes forward about a sexual assault.

Another factor that contributes to doubt about rape accusations is the idea that rapists are always weird or creepy people. In reality, many rapists are charming and loved by their friends and family—and, in the case of celebrities, even loved by people who have never met them. When a woman comes forward to accuse a seemingly normal man or beloved celebrity of sexual assault, it is common for people to say the woman must be lying because they have a hard time reconciling their love for this person with the idea that he committed such a terrible act. This is one of the contradictions of rape culture: Rape is widely considered to be one of the worst crimes a person can commit, yet people often dismiss it because they do not know how to feel when they find out someone they admire has committed it.

Modern Problems

The Rape, Abuse, and Incest National Network (RAINN), the largest anti–sexual violence organization in the United States, estimates that an American is sexually assaulted every 98 seconds. One out of every six American women has been the victim of attempted or completed rape at some point in their lives, as has one out of every thirty-three American men. Some call rape in the United States an epidemic, with more people being sexually assaulted every year than being hospitalized with the flu. Although sexual assault has dropped by 63 percent since 1993 and the U.S. government has, in the past, tried to address the issue, nothing in the past two decades has succeeded in stopping sexual crimes in a significant way. Rape culture makes it seem as though sexual violence is a natural part of life, and society's inability to change the statistics may seem to back up that belief, but the problems in Western society that allow rape to continue are difficult to solve quickly and all at once. Ultimately, examining the issues and being aware of each individual's part in them is the first step toward making bigger changes.

A Universal Problem

Rape culture is something that affects everyone. Although the conversation generally focuses on women, men can be victims of sexual assault as well. Between 5 and 14 percent of reported rapes are against men and boys, so while they are statistically less likely to be assaulted, it is also not completely uncommon. In contrast to the privilege men have in most situations, male victims are some of the most invisible and receive little to no support from the public, including law enforcement. The National Alliance to End Sexual Violence speculated on why that might be:

For our society to acknowledge that men are raped, we must first rec-
ognize and acknowledge that men can be vulnerable. Both men and
women are socialized to see men as powerful, assertive and in control
of their bodies. It may be challenging for some to think of men being
the victims of sexual crimes because it is challenging to recognize men
as "victims" and still think of them as men. This socialization can
make it less likely for men to seek services and can make it less likely
that appropriate services are available.[12]

In a society that bases masculinity on physical strength and
emotional inflexibility, many people believe it is impossible for
men to be sexually assaulted, and if they are assaulted, it is often
believed that they clearly are not manly enough and therefore deserved it; male victims may be asked more frequently than female
victims why they did not fight back against their attacker, implying that if they were strong enough, they would not have been
raped. In other cases, specifically those involving female perpetrators, male victims are often congratulated instead of comforted
because of the stereotype that men are obsessed with sex and will
enjoy it no matter what. Not only is this stereotype not true, it
also creates a hostile social environment when male rape survivors
challenge it.

Another overlooked group is the LGBT+ community. Across the
board, gay, lesbian, and bisexual people have a greater chance of experiencing sexual violence than heterosexual people, with bisexual
women having the highest rate of incidence—46 percent—of any
of these groups. Transgender people also have alarmingly high rates
for receiving sexual abuse, with different sources estimating between
50 and 66 percent of trans people having been assaulted at some
point in their lives. RAINN reports that 21 percent of transgender
and nonbinary college students have been victimized. Looking at
these statistics, it becomes clear that because LGBT+ individuals are
already marginalized, or ignored by mainstream society, sex offend-
ers see them as easy targets. Without the support of the community,
it is less likely that abusers will be reported and caught.

People of color also have a more elevated risk of sexual assault than their white counterparts. In the United States, the only
marginalized racial group to have a lesser chance of being a victim
of rape than white women are Asian and Pacific Islander women.

The intersection of sexual assault and racism is historical, going all the way back to the early days of what is now the United States, when Native American women were raped by European colonists and African women were raped by the white men who kept them as slaves. A great deal of the sexual assault that goes on today is an extension of that, as a way of maintaining racial dominance. Native American and African American women continue to be the most likely victims of rape or attempted rape during their lifetimes. Sexual violence, in general, is often about gaining power over the victim and is very rarely only an act of lust, but the assault of people of color is a piece of the wider problem of racism in the United States.

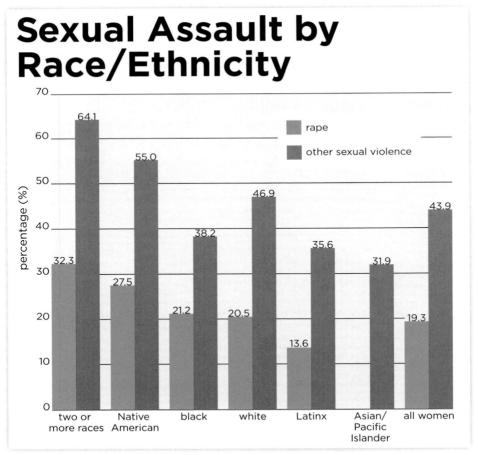

Although all women face the possibility of rape or sexual violence, women of color often suffer more frequently than white women, as this information from the Institute for Women's Policy Research shows.

Corrective Rape

Charity workers in South Africa coined the term "corrective rape" to describe the systematic sexual assault of South African lesbians at the hands of men who want to "cure" them of their homosexuality. The country already has one of the highest rates of rape in the world, but during its recent shift to democracy, forcing women into gender-specific roles such as wife and mother became a way to maintain power over them. Lesbians are seen as major threats to male power because they do not have a male head of household, so many men have taken it upon themselves to "fix" them.

This phenomenon is not exclusive to South Africa or to lesbians. Once the term "corrective rape" became widely known, LGBT+ people all over the world began to talk about their own experiences being sexually assaulted in an attempt to change who they are. One group that is particularly likely to have this done to them is the asexual community. Asexuals, who do not experience sexual attraction, are often guilted into sex by their romantic partners or raped in a useless attempt to "make them like it." However, recent media exposure of this underrepresented group may help make a difference in how they are treated in the future.

Blaming the Victim

When sexual assault cases go to court and come under the media spotlight, a common comment from the public is that the victim must have provoked their attacker or done something to deserve it. People believe sexual assault happens only if the victim is not careful, but the guidelines of what not to do are very restrictive. Even though it has been proven that rape happens regardless of what the victim is wearing, women are told not to wear revealing clothes, even in the summer. Shorts, tank tops, and dresses are all considered bait and are probably the most commonly used excuse for sexual assault. Women are also advised not to drink alcohol in public places such as parties or bars because intoxication limits their ability to consent. Going out at night, wearing makeup, and even talking to men in general are also named as "reasons" women are assaulted. It often seems as if anything a woman does is enough for her to be molested and have other people blame her—instead of her attacker—for it.

Psychologists believe people on the outside of a situation involving assault have this reaction because of something known as the "just world hypothesis," or the idea in society that people get what they deserve. In an analysis of victim-blaming, Dr. Juliana Breines explained:

> Victims threaten our sense that the world is a safe and moral place, where good things happen to good people and bad things happen to bad people. When bad things happen to good people, it implies that no one is safe, that no matter how good we are, we too could be vulnerable. The idea that misfortune can be random, striking anyone at any time, is a terrifying thought, and yet we are faced every day with evidence that it may be true.[13]

The idea that the world is fair assures people that if they take the right precautions, they will not be harmed, but victims of all types remind people that the world is not always fair. Blaming a rape victim for not being careful enough relieves the fear of vulnerability for onlookers, but it does not help the victim or ensure that future victims will come forward.

Being blamed for such a traumatic event can have serious psychological effects. In the aftermath of their assault, rape victims are likely to blame themselves because they have been raised in a society that emphasizes the "just world theory" the same way everyone else around them has, but having that feeling of blame validated by other people can make it much worse. Victims of sexual assault are prone to depression and PTSD, both of which can lead to dissociation—feeling disconnected from one's body—and self-harm. Without support, some of these effects can become life-threatening, and victim-blaming is the very opposite of support.

Victim-blaming can be hard to shut out, especially when it validates a victim's fears and guilt.

Fear in Reporting

Statistics estimate that only about 15 to 35 percent of all sexual assaults are reported to the police. Victims who do report their assault believe reporting will improve their situation—they believe the perpetrator will be caught and held accountable—but the relatively low number of reports suggests that more people believe telling the authorities will do nothing or make the situation worse. This is what rape culture tells victims: In many different ways, society discourages reporting rape or sexual assault, sometimes with outright punishment for speaking up. With that as the case, it is important to examine the roots of the reasons why victims do not report their sexual assault and work to remove the social obstacles that get in the way of justice.

Some sexual assault survivors fear retaliation, or revenge, for reporting their attack. In the military, where sexual assault is 50 to 100 percent more likely to happen than in the rest of America, the threat of retaliation for reporting comes from multiple places. In 2011, Airman Jessica Hinves was honorably discharged from the air force because of a diagnosis of PTSD after she was assaulted by someone on her command team. Before this, a ranking officer had told her he could not guarantee her safety on the base, and by the time of her discharge, her fellow airmen had all turned against her because she was "ruining" her attacker's career. After speaking out publicly in a documentary, the military itself turned against her as well. She received a new diagnosis from air force medical staff of borderline personality disorder (BPD)—a mental illness that affects about 1.6 percent of the population and is often misused to dismiss cases of military sexual assault—and her benefits were decreased significantly. Although she took her case to court and was awarded more benefits later, the problem lies in the military's reaction to her reporting. Not only did her fellow airmen reject her, but the entire air force system became hostile against her, taking away her benefits because she did not keep quiet about her attack. Because of stories like Hinves's, about 80 percent of assault victims in the military never step forward.

NEGATIVE REINFORCEMENT

"Victim-blaming attitudes also reinforce what the abuser has been saying all along; that it is the victim's fault this is happening. It is NOT the victim's fault or responsibility to fix the situation; it is the abuser's choice. By engaging in victim-blaming attitudes, society allows the abuser to perpetrate relationship abuse or sexual assault while avoiding accountability for those actions."

–Center for Relationship Abuse Awareness

"Avoiding Victim Blaming," Center for Relationship Abuse Awareness, 2015. stoprelationshipabuse. org/educated/avoiding-victim-blaming/.

Another reason assault victims do not go to the police is because they believe the police will not help them. Even though the victims of any crime should always feel safe going to the police, police departments have often shown that they do not take sexual assault seriously. In Baltimore, for example, a 2016

After her ordeal in the air force, Jessica Hinves (middle) *took part in the documentary* The Invisible War, *produced by Amy Ziering* (left) *and directed by Kirby Dick* (right). *The film attempted to shed light on the crisis of sexual assault in the military and won a Peabody Award and an Emmy for Best Documentary Feature and Outstanding Investigative Journalism.*

report from the U.S. Justice Department described the local police department as "grossly inadequate" when it came to investigating rape cases. "Baltimore officers sometimes humiliated women who tried to report sexual assault," explained journalists from the *New York Times*, "often failed to gather basic evidence, and disregarded some complaints filed by prostitutes. Some officers blamed victims or discouraged them from identifying their assailants, asking questions like, 'Why are you messing that guy's life up?'"[14] In a perfect world, police officers would look beyond their own cultural biases when upholding the law, but the reality is that police are equally as likely to dismiss a sexual assault as many other misinformed people. Rape victims require support if they are going to press charges, but finding that support, even from the authorities, can be too difficult for them to want to follow through.

For some people, not getting their attacker in trouble is their biggest priority. This generally happens when the perpetrator is someone the victim knows, such as a family member or a friend. A myth about sexual assault is that it is done by random strangers; the reality is that 7 out of every 10 acts of sexual violence are committed by someone known to the victim, even if only by acquaintance. Only 18 to 40 percent of these assaults, however, are reported. In these cases, victims are more likely to brush off the assault because of their personal relationship with their attacker. Even in cases where the person does not know the attacker well, Western society perpetuates the idea that a charge of rape will ruin a man's life and that this is an unfair punishment, even if the rape accusation is not false. This is one of the only crimes where people believe it is unfair for a guilty person to serve jail time for the crime they were proven to have committed. This may be partially because of the false but enduring idea that men are not responsible for their actions when they become sexually aroused. Many people believe that if a woman is wearing a particular outfit or acting in a particular way and a man is sexually attracted to her, the rape is her fault, not his. By taking this view, they see harsh punishment as unfair to the man. However, the truth is that rape is a choice that a rapist willingly makes; men are not unable to control themselves, and rape is never a victim's fault. Additionally, other crimes are not viewed the same way. For example, if a person was arrested for robbing a store and their defense was that the merchandise looked too good to resist, people would generally not agree that the robber cannot be held responsible.

In some cases, sexual assault or harrassment is not reported because the victim does not understand its importance. In the workplace, sexual harassment is a chargeable offense, but it goes unreported 75 percent of the time. Not only is this because so many of these claims are either not investigated or are thrown out because they are unable to be verified, it also has to do with how seriously the victim takes it. Someone could be sexually harassed and feel that they do not need to report it because it did not become physical, even though verbal harassment is illegal as well. Making light of harassment opens the door to making light of assault, something that prevents rape victims from getting the help they need.

The Justice System

Although the U.S. justice system is designed to punish criminals, perpetrators of sexual harassment, sexual assault, and rape rarely face the consequences of their actions. According to the U.S. Department of Justice, only 310 out of 1,000 rapes are ever reported to the police, 57 of which lead to arrests. Of those 57 arrests, only 11 cases will be referred to prosecutors, and 7 of those 11 cases will result in a felony conviction. Only 6 out of every 1,000 rapists ever see time in prison. With these staggering statistics in mind, a legitimate question arises: How are so many criminals slipping through the cracks?

Even if a victim of sexual violence defies the odds and decides to go to the police, issues begin as soon as they give their report. Some police departments will dismiss sexual assault reports right from the start, although many are sympathetic and will begin with an interview of the victim. The interview process can be emotionally and mentally exhausting for someone who has been through a trauma such as rape, but it is necessary for the investigation. This is where victim-blaming sometimes happens, when the victim is cross-examined as a criminal would be.

Another early part of a sexual assault investigation is sometimes a medical examination. These are common when a sexual assault has occurred within 72 hours because the evidence is fresh. During the forensic exam, a nurse or other trained medical professional uses what is called a Sexual Assault Evidence Kit (SAEK), sometimes known as a "rape kit." At their smallest, these include containers and swabs for collecting evidence and documentation forms, but they may also come with things such as a comb and materials for blood sampling. In the United States, however, these kits become a problem because of what is known as the rape kit backlog. Hundreds of thousands of rape kits go untested. In some cases, detectives do not ask for DNA analysis, so the kits remain in storage, and in other cases, the crime lab, for whatever reason, does not prioritize the kits and can take more than 30 days to test them. Either way, the backlog makes sexual assault investigations much more difficult because a large piece of the evidence puzzle is missing.

994 of 1000 Perpetrators of Rape Walk Free

310 are reported to the police.

57 reports lead to arrest.

11 cases get referred to prosecutors.

7 cases will lead to a felony conviction.

6 rapists will be incarcerated.

As rape cases go through the criminal justice system, more and more are dropped for one reason or another. This makes it very difficult for survivors to get their attackers off the streets, as this information from RAINN shows.

Although a rape kit is supposed to ease the burden on the victim, it can sometimes cause a different problem. In 2015, Congress reauthorized an existing law called the Violence Against Women Act, which stated that rape victims are not to be charged for their rape kit and any medical treatment they receive—for instance, medication to protect against an HIV infection. However, despite this law, some women are still charged for these things, even if they have health insurance. Often this is a result of an error on the part of a hospital's billing department, and the charge may be able to be reversed in this case. Other times, the problem is confusion about what the law covers. For example, although some states cover pregnancy tests, others do not. Additionally, some health insurance policies will not pay for all the tests and treatment a rape victim may need. The news website Reuters reported that victims with insurance still pay about 14 percent of their medical costs—an average of $950. This would not be the case if the person had been the victim of a different kind of violent crime. For this reason, a woman may choose to decline a rape kit if she cannot afford to pay for it.

If the preliminary evidence is gathered, the decision to continue the investigation must be made. RAINN goes into detail about this process and the ways it could be put on hold:

> After the initial report is made to law enforcement, a survivor can decide whether or not they would like to move forward with the investigation, a process referred to as pressing charges. Ultimately, the decision to press criminal charges is up to the state ... If law enforcement or the prosecution team feel that they are not able to prove guilt, they may decide not to press charges. They may have encountered challenges proving the case due to a lack of evidence, an inability to identify the perpetrator, or other factors.[15]

This is how those 310 reported sexual assaults are shaved down to only the 11 that ever reach the court system. With so many untested rape kits, however, it is unsurprising that so many cases are thrown out because of a lack of evidence or the inability to identify the attacker. In this way, the rape kit backlog and the financial cost contribute to rape culture by considerably reducing the number of perpetrators who are caught. Allowing rapists to walk free makes sexual assault seem easy to get away with, creating a culture of people who do not understand how serious sexual violence is.

Going to Court

There are three different ways a sexual assault case could go through the court system. When law enforcement decides not to prosecute, a victim may look for justice by filing a civil suit. "The civil justice system does not attempt to determine the innocence or guilt of an offender," according to the National Center for Victims of Crime. "Rather, it attempts to determine whether an offender or a third party is liable for the injuries sustained as a result of the crime."[16] If a sexual assault survivor wins in civil court, their attacker must pay them, essentially, for the damage they caused. Overall, a civil suit tends to give the victim more control over the case, and it also holds the perpetrator accountable directly to the victim.

If a sexual assault case is taken on by law enforcement, it becomes what is known as "a crime against the state." In these cases, the state—meaning the government—is in control of the case and the victim, as a witness, is simply a piece of evidence. Many criminal court assault cases are settled through a plea bargain, or "an agreement between the prosecutor and perpetrator's representative, in which the perpetrator agrees to plead guilty to a crime in return for a reduction in penalty, such as a lighter sentence. This course of action does not involve or require the survivor to testify."[17] This route does not result in a trial, which is why the victim does not have to testify. A case like this is arguably easier on the victim, but it does not send a strong message.

In criminal cases that do not end in a plea bargain, however, the matter is taken to court in front of a jury. Here, the victim is likely to have to testify against their attacker and tell their story to the judge, jury, and news media. At this point, the victim is generally as much on trial as the perpetrator, although not literally. Not only are they cross-examined to find out if they are lying, they are on display for everyone to have an opinion about. The news media reports the details of the trial to the public, and the public acts like a second jury, deciding who they believe is at fault for the assault before the trial ends. During most criminal sexual assault trials that make headline news, the public is split between those who support the victim and those who support the perpetrator, and being the center of so much controversy can be extremely difficult for a survivor seeking justice. Even judges get caught up in the public debate, and a few have gone so far as to express their personal opinions in court despite how inappropriate their comments are. Again, a victim might find themselves not believed by the authorities, and this time the authority is the person most responsible for punishing the perpetrator of their assault. Not only does this harm the current victim, who has to live through being publicly shamed by a judge, but it also discourages future victims from seeking help from the criminal justice system at all.

Celebrity Power

Celebrity scandals are nothing new, but the ones most likely to still inspire shock are those involving sexual assault. In only the past few years, rape and sexual harassment allegations have been brought against President Donald Trump, comedian Bill Cosby, and former FOX News CEO Roger Ailes and anchor Bill O'Reilly. Most recently, Harvey Weinstein, a film producer who helped found the major film studio Miramax, has been accused by dozens of women of sexual harrassment and assault. This proves that the "casting couch mentality" of Hollywood—a phrase used to describe aspiring actors and actresses trading sexual favors for acting parts, often because of pressure from executives—is all too real. Many of the people who were affected by Weinstein's actions, including Gwyneth Paltrow and Angelina Jolie, felt pressured to keep the incidents secret and even maintained a seemingly friendly relationship with Weinstein for the sake of their careers.

Few of these accusations, however, have resulted in any real, legal consequences. Cosby admitted to drugging and assaulting a number of women, yet remains out of jail. Although Ailes and O'Reilly lost their jobs, they both left FOX with millions of dollars in their pockets and loyal followings of fans. Weinstein was fired by Miramax, but many of the sexual assault incidents may have happened too long ago for him to suffer legal consequences. Trump was elected president of the United States. Author Nathan J. Robinson said this about how the rich and powerful remain above the law:

> Everyone knows that the wealthy and famous can get away with things that would land other people in prison ... Yet this is the way wealth works: it confers a kind of total impunity, in which no amount of evidence is enough to make anything matter. Some of that impunity comes from the ability to use money to buy people and lawyers to intimidate them ... But this is not just a story about lawyers. It is also about complicity: the complicity of large institutions, and of the public at large, in refusing to hold these men accountable.[18]

Robinson points the finger at society. With so little understanding about how serious sexual assault is and so little concern for how survivors feel, as well as the culture-wide worship of celebrities and fame, it is no wonder that society allows these men to get away with hurting people. In the same way that many assume rape victims must have done something wrong to have allowed themselves to be raped, Western culture tells people that rich people must be good because good things, such as becoming rich, have happened to them. This is, unfortunately, often untrue in reality.

Donald Trump's comments about touching women without their consent and the accusations of sexual assault that arose during his presidential campaign did not prevent people from voting for him because they believed other issues were more important. Attitudes such as this help reinforce rape culture.

Since the accusations about Weinstein have come to light, other male celebrities have lost their jobs after facing similar accusations. Some people are happy to see sexual harassers finally facing consequences, while others have continued to claim that these men do not deserve to be fired for their behavior or that the stories must be false because there are too many of them coming out at once. In reality, it is likely that victims are gaining the courage to speak up now that harassers are facing consequences. Some people see this as a sign that positive change is happening.

Campus Assault

Surveys estimate that 11.2 percent of all college students are the victims of sexual assault. Among undergraduates, 23.1 percent of women and 5.4 percent of men experience sexual violence at the hands of their peers, yet many colleges remain unprepared and sometimes unwilling to act against it. When a rape or sexual assault is reported to a college, the investigation falls into the laps of the campus disciplinary board, the members of which are often unqualified to handle a case that should be dealt with by the police. From there, the members of the college board serve as the ultimate authorities. Without lawyers present, panelists' biases rule the investigation, resulting in unhelpful lines of questioning and uneven examination of evidence. Keeping up appearances often becomes the bottom line—the reputation of the school is at stake if the disciplinary board makes a mistake—so many cases are dropped simply because the college does not want to look bad.

In recent years, two campus rape cases have taken center stage in the conversation about sexual assault in colleges. The first began in 2013, at Columbia University in New York City. Emma Sulkowicz, then a sophomore, accused her friend, Paul Nungesser, of rape and reported it to the university only to have Nungesser cleared of the charges. A year and a half later, Sulkowicz started her senior year and her senior thesis, a social experiment and performance art piece now known as *Mattress Performance (Carry That Weight)*. From her first day of classes to graduation day, she carried a twin-sized dorm mattress everywhere with her on campus to make the pain carried by rape survivors visible. She attracted major media attention and gained the support of many women's advocate groups, but in the process she drew unwelcome public attention to Nungesser. In April 2015, he sued Columbia for gender discrimination, claiming that the school was inadvertently supporting a public campaign against him, but the case was dismissed. Here, the university was caught between two students, and without the proper resources to make an informed investigation, there is no way to know who was telling the truth. The carried mattress, however, has become a powerful symbol of visibility and unity for victims of sexual assault. In an interview conducted not long after she carried the mattress across the graduation stage, Sulkowicz commented, "To me, the piece has very much represented [the fact that] a guy did a horrible thing to me and I tried to make something beautiful out of it."[19]

Emma Sulkowicz is shown here with the mattress she carried around Columbia University for nine months.

The second case happened at Stanford University in California. In January 2015, two Stanford graduate students were riding their bikes across the campus when they saw Brock Turner on top of an unconscious young woman by a dumpster. When Turner tried to run, one of the students chased him down and wrestled him to the ground to wait for the police. Turner claimed the young woman had given consent, but she reported

"Distorted Beyond Recognition"

In contrast to Brock Turner's father's letter, the victim of the Stanford rape case, who remained anonymous, made a statement to the court before Turner was given his light sentence. For most of her speech, she spoke directly to Turner and described the effect his assault had on her life:

> My independence, natural joy, gentleness, and steady lifestyle I had been enjoying became distorted beyond recognition. I became closed off, angry, self-deprecating, tired, irritable, empty. The isolation at times was unbearable. You cannot give me back the life I had before that night either. While you worry about your shattered reputation, I refrigerated spoons every night so when I woke up, and my eyes were puffy from crying, I would hold the spoons to my eyes to lessen the swelling so that I could see. I showed up an hour late to work every morning, excused myself to cry in the stairwells, I can tell you all the best places in that building to cry where no one can hear you. ... I can't sleep alone at night without having a light on, like a five-year-old, because I have nightmares of being touched where I cannot wake up, I did this thing where I waited until the sun came up and I felt safe enough to sleep. For three months, I went to bed at six o'clock in the morning.[1]

1. Anonymous, statement posted by Katie J.M. Baker, "Here Is the Powerful Letter the Stanford Victim Read Aloud to Her Attacker," Buzzfeed News, June 3, 2016. www.buzzfeed.com/katiejmbaker/heres-the-powerful-letter-the-stanford-victim-read-to-her-rs?utm_term=.mjRXgBaEG#.dlp2EqoeM

having no memory of the encounter; both had been to a party that night and were intoxicated. The fact that she had been unconscious, however, made it clear that she could not have given consent even if Turner had asked.

The trial went on for over a year. Journalist Marina Koren wrote in *The Atlantic*,

> *Turner faced up to 14 years in state prison when he was convicted in March of three felonies—assault with intent to commit rape of an intoxicated woman, sexually penetrating an intoxicated person with a foreign object, and sexually penetrating an unconscious person with a foreign object—and prosecutors had asked for six years. But the judge had ordered much less, saying a harsher sentence would have a "severe impact" on Turner, a star swimmer who could have made it to the Olympics.*[20]

In the end, Turner received six months in jail and three years of probation, and he served only three months of his sentence before being released.

The Stanford case was not so much a showcase of the university's handling of the crime as it was a good example of how the media handles such a crime. Throughout the trial, Turner was written and spoken about in the media as a star athlete who, it was implied, happened to make a minor mistake. Meanwhile, the same media outlets emphasized that the woman he had assaulted was drunk, implying the assault would not have happened if she were sober. During criminal rape trials, especially ones involving college students, it is common to see male perpetrators portrayed as upstanding young men with their bright futures on the line, while female victims—often students themselves, with equally bright futures now darkened by the emotional, mental, and sometimes physical damage caused by being sexually assaulted—are portrayed as vindictive liars or drunken idiots. In a letter to the court, Turner's father referred to his son's attempted rape of an unconscious woman as "20 minutes of action,"[21] objectifying the young woman and trying to minimize the violence of the rape by mentioning how little time it had taken.

A Harmful Cycle

It is very rare that someone openly and honestly says something such as, "I believe women deserve to be raped." People who believe something like that are more likely to say, "Look at what she was wearing," or "She was asking for it," implying their meaning without really saying it. This is how most cultural beliefs are expressed; people are commonly unaware of the underlying meaning of what they say because they picked it up unconsciously from their parents or from other people around them.

People learn most of their culture when they are very young. Cultural learning is generally done without people realizing they are doing it, by observing what their parents do and what they say. This is called modeling. Cultural teaching is sometimes equally subconscious for parents, who often do not realize that everything they do and say has an impact on their children. As people get older, the things they learned as children get reinforced by multiple sources. Sometimes, when their views align with the values and beliefs that are widely popular, society confirms them. Other times, when their views do not match up, people find various ways to confirm their own views. One of these is called confirmation bias, when they seek out and remember information that confirms their beliefs and ignore information that does not. In either situation, their own personal ideas about how culture should operate are strengthened.

This is how rape culture gets perpetuated. Toxic ideas—including that sexual violence is normal, that women are inferior to men, and that people get what they deserve—have been passed down through many generations, but they benefit no one except a select, privileged few. Passing down these ideas again will only cause more harm in the future, so recognizing the ways society reinforces rape culture is very important if things are going to change.

The Patriarchal Structure

In social studies, the word "patriarchy" is taught to mean a society in which men are the heads of their families and inheritance is only passed down from father to son, through the male line. However, this definition ignores the way a male-centered household affects the entire culture. Because men are considered more valuable in a society where they lead the family, they are born with more power and influence than women, and this ultimately causes the society to value masculinity over femininity. Modern American culture has taken steps away from a patriarchal family structure in recent years—more families have an equal share of power between parents or have only one parent to begin with—but people often still treat men and women differently, and these differences contribute to rape culture in small ways that add up.

In a patriarchy, gender differences matter; they are the foundation on which a patriarchy is built. People are split into the gender binary, a system where there are only two genders based on biological sex. The gender binary ignores two important facts right from the beginning. First, there is a range of biological sexes based on the number of sex chromosomes, X and Y, a person has in their genetic structure. Second, gender has little or nothing to do with biological sex. Regardless, the gender binary puts people into two boxes, male and female, and labels them as opposites of each other. Men are expected to be independent, nonemotional, aggressive, tough-skinned, competitive, and physically strong, automatically making women dependent, emotional, submissive, thin-skinned, unambitious, and physically weak. Masculine traits are highly prized, while feminine traits are looked down upon. This is how men maintain their position of power and create the patriarchal structure. Trans and nonbinary people also feel the pressure to fit into these roles, but they are often shunned because their very existence challenges the roots of the gender binary.

The devaluing of feminine traits is damaging to men, women, and everyone in between. A patriarchal society such as the United States has traditionally demonized anyone who seems too feminine; men who are emotional or unambitious may be shamed for being "unmanly," and women who are too dependent or physically weak may be made to feel like burdens. However, for men, it does not go the same way with masculine traits. Traditonally, a man could never be too tough or competitive, but a woman who is unemotional or tough-skinned is seen as cold and heartless. There is a difference between society's values and individual values; some people may reject these views, and many are actively working to change them, with some success. However, others hold onto these outdated views. When women are the subject of so much disapproval and sometimes downright hatred, it makes them targets for violence of all kinds, including sexual assault; and when men are taught to be aggressive and dominant, it makes them more likely to commit those violent acts.

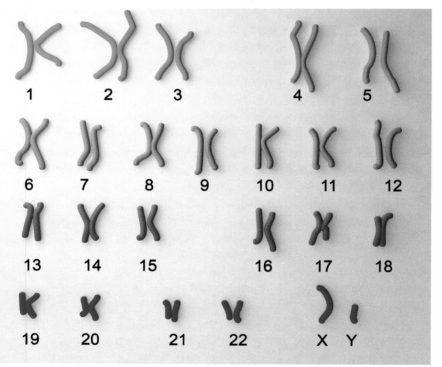

Humans have 23 pairs of chromosomes, including the sex chromosomes X and Y. Scientists once thought that only the combinations XY (for a male) and XX (for a female) were normal, but recent studies have found that there are many different combinations, such as XXY and XYY, that occur naturally.

A MALE PERSPECTIVE

"The problem is that I have never felt at home in groups predominately comprised of white men. I can trace that back to my childhood when I spent much of my time being mercilessly bullied by my white male peers. Whether it was my sensitivity, willingness to listen and share my feelings or my proclivity for picking up a book before tossing around a football, I've never fitted into the box of stereotypical masculinity."

—Marc Peters, author of "Reflecting on the Oppressor in the Mirror"

Marc Peters, "Reflecting on the Oppressor in the Mirror," *IDS Bulletin*, vol. 45, no. 1 (January 2014): pp. 99-100. bulletin.ids.ac.uk/idsbo/article/view/188.

The Way Kids Play

Ideas about gender are taught at a very young age, but most people probably could not pinpoint exactly when or how. Like most social learning, gender roles are taught through reinforcement. When a parent or other adult encourages or discourages an action again and again, a child will tend to pick up the pattern and behave the way they have been told to.

On the playground, boys and girls are equally as likely to run, jump, and climb if given the chance, but not all children are allowed to play in the same ways once a parent steps in. While boys are encouraged to climb higher and run faster than their peers, girls are often discouraged from doing so even if they are physically equal to the boys. In general, the boys are praised for playing dangerously, for leaping across gaps and swinging wildly from the monkey bars, but the girls are often told to get down when they climb too high. By treating the children differently, their parents are teaching them very different things: The boys learn to take risks and to be more aggressive, and the girls learn about danger—that climbing up where the boys go is somehow more dangerous for them simply because of their gender. This might make some of them more timid and less ambitious in the long run.

Kids love playing together on the playground, but the way their parents treat them based on their assigned genders can change how they interact with the world and each other.

For the BBC Two documentary *No More Boys and Girls: Can Our Kids Go Gender Free?*, Dr. Javid Abdelmoneim set up a small experiment to see how adults played with toddlers of different assigned genders when given a variety of toys. To further his point, he swapped the children's clothes and gave each of them a new, obviously gendered name for the duration of the experiment. Marnie became Oliver and Edward became Sophie, and then they were handed off to volunteers for playtime. "Sophie," who was assigned male at birth, was offered exclusively pink stuffed animals and baby dolls when the volunteers believed he was a girl, even though many other kinds of toys were available. While these kinds of toys might teach nurturing behavior, they are passive—they do not require skills to play with—and they do not contribute very much to a little girl's development at that age. "Oliver," on the other hand, was given puzzle games, a plastic robot, and a ride on a toy car. When the volunteers believed they were playing with a little boy, they were more interactive, allowing "him" more opportunities to practice motor and spatial skills. Other researchers believe adults show gender bias even around newborns, which means babies are quite literally born into the gender binary.

Children's interests are often influenced by the gender roles adults reinforce, but given freedom from society's expectations, children of all genders enjoy things such as space, animals, and dinosaurs.

Nature or Nurture?

For a long time, scientists of all kinds assumed the differences between men and women were natural, there from birth, and unchangeable. New research, however, is challenging that idea and suggests that many of the differences seen in how men and women behave are because of how they were raised. Scientists now know that the human brain has a quality called plasticity, meaning it can be shaped by experiences and changes drastically as people grow up. For example, researchers found that a part of the brain that controls social thinking and judgment, which is generally larger in adult women and seems to be the reason why women tend to be more sensitive toward other people, is actually larger in young boys than girls. Lise Eliot, a professor of neuroscience at Rosalind Franklin University, explained:

> Yes, men and women are psychologically different and yes, neuroscientists are uncovering many differences in brain anatomy and physiology which seem to explain our behavioral differences. But just because a difference is biological doesn't mean it is "hard-wired." Individuals' gender traits—their preference for masculine or feminine clothes, careers, hobbies and interpersonal styles—are inevitably shaped more by rearing and experience than is their biological sex. Likewise, their brains, which are ultimately producing all this masculine or feminine behavior, must be molded—at least to some degree—by the sum of their experiences as a boy or girl.[1]

1. Lise Eliot, "Girl Brain, Boy Brain?," *Scientific American*, September 8, 2009. www.scientificamerican.com/article/girl-brain-boy-brain/

Why do adults behave this way with children? Some believe the gender binary is a natural system for humans, even though science disagrees. Others simply do not think about it at all; they raise their children the way they were raised without considering shifting ideas about gender. If asked about it, they might say they want their children to fit in. If their son is too "girly," the other boys might make fun of him, and if their daughter is too "boyish," she might not be accepted by the other girls. There is also the fear that behavior too far outside the gender binary means the child is LGBT+, which for some parents is still unthinkable. Whatever the reason, the fact remains that strictly enforcing gender roles creates unrealistic standards of behavior and can, in some cases, psychologically harm a child who feels they do not fit into the mold.

How the Media Shapes Culture

The media plays a large role in how people view sexual assault, but it does very little to change the conversation. To appeal to the widest audience, both news and entertainment media rarely take controversial stances on anything, instead playing the middle ground so they do not offend people on either side of an issue. In situations when rape comes to the forefront, the media generally remains neutral, even though being neutral about sexual violence actually helps it continue.

When a sexual assault case is being talked about on the news, it is likely that the reporters will subtly take the side of the offender. As in the Stanford rape case, men who attack women and get caught are often said to be having their lives ruined, while the victim is interrogated and harassed because they came forward. Alyssa, a 19-year-old rape survivor, commented, "The news treats victims [poorly]. I was scared to come out because I've seen what's happened to girls like me. They get death threats, rape threats. It's like they have to face even more bad stuff because they were brave and they spoke up. That's not okay."[22] When the news stands with the perpetrator of a sex crime, it tells the rest of society that this is the correct side to be on.

Even entertainment media, such as TV shows and movies, often send a harmful message when they are trying to be part of the solution. For example, *Law and Order: Special Victims Unit* is a show that deals with sexual assault crimes, and it serves as one of the only voices of regular support for rape victims on television. Unfortunately, the series often reinforces the idea that the victims caused their assault in some way and uses language such as "idiotic" or "slutty" to describe the victim. Even though the show has good intentions, it ends up reaffirming the false

"I Know You Want It"

In 2013, R&B singer Robin Thicke's song "Blurred Lines" stirred up controversy among rape survivors and women's advocacy groups all over the world. Although Pharrell Williams, who produced the song, denied that it was about sex, the lyrics suggest otherwise. Some felt there was nothing wrong with the song, believing the lyrics were about a man and a woman clearly flirting with each other. However, others believed the song clearly had a predatory aspect. In particular, rape and sexual assault survivors were offended by the line, "I know you want it,"[1] which many said was disturbingly close to something their rapists had said to them. The song made it to the top of the charts, but it was so hated because of its "rapey"[2] implications that some student unions at universities banned the song from being played at social functions on campus. Kirsty Haigh, vice president of the Edinburgh University Students' Association, commented, "The song says: 'You know you want it.' Well, you can't know they want it unless they tell you they want it."[3] Even though the song was obviously inappropriate, it brought the conversation about consent to the forefront of the media for a few months, making more people aware of one of the biggest problems with rape culture than had probably ever thought about it before.

1. Robin Thicke, "Blurred Lines," Star Trak. Originally released March 20, 2013.

2. Tricia Romano, "'Blurred Lines,' Robin Thicke's Summer Anthem, Is Kind of Rapey," *Daily Beast*, June 17, 2013. www.thedailybeast.com/blurred-lines-robin-thickes-summer-anthem-is-kind-of-rapey.

3. Quoted in Dorian Lynskey, "Blurred Lines: The Most Controversial Song of the Decade," *Guardian*, November 13, 2013. www.theguardian.com/music/2013/nov/13/blurred-lines-most-controversial-song-decade.

things people already believe about sexual violence, and many shows and movies dealing with the same topic fall into the same pattern. Ultimately, representation similar to this does not help survivors cope nor does it inform the public, making it part of the problem.

Rape Jokes

The way people talk about rape has an impact on how they and the people around them see it, and joking about it makes it seem less serious than it is. Using the word in casual conversation—for example, "I got raped by that test," or "I raped you at that game"—normalizes the idea of rape even if it was not meant literally. One consequence of using that kind of language is that it is insulting to rape survivors—and since many people do not talk about their experiences with rape, people may be talking to a rape survivor without even realizing it. Additionally, it allows sexual abusers to continue believing that what they are doing to people is an acceptable thing to do. Rapists often believe that everyone has the potential to be a rapist—that given a chance, anyone would do what they have done—so talking about rape in a light manner gives them the impression that what they believe is true.

Comedians, especially male ones, often find it ridiculous that there are things they should not joke about. Many comedians believe nothing is off limits for a joke and become incredibly defensive when someone points out that what they are joking about is hurting people. They claim that the "thought police" are censoring them when rape victims and their supporters tell comedians they are being insensitive. In her article "How to Make a Rape Joke," Lindy West suggested that there are ways to joke about horrible things, but the comedians who are fighting against "censorship" are missing the point:

> If people don't want to be offended, they shouldn't go to comedy clubs? Maybe. But if you don't want people to react to your jokes, you shouldn't get on stage and tell your jokes to people ... You can be edgy and creepy and offensive and trivial and, yes, you can talk about rape. But if you want people to not hate you (and wanting

to not be hated is not the same thing as wanting to be liked), you should probably try and do it in a responsible, thoughtful way. Easy shortcut: DO NOT MAKE RAPE VICTIMS THE BUTT OF THE JOKE.[23]

In other words, it is not illegal to make a rape joke, but people are also not required to silently accept those jokes or pretend they find them funny. Many people do not appreciate jokes about rape victims or the act of rape itself—for instance, joking about how drugging a girl would be the only way for a comedian to get one to come home with him. These jokes openly perpetuate rape culture, and if the comedian gets fired for making a joke like that or if people choose not to go to their shows, it is not an assault on the comedian's right to free speech; it is a reaction from other people who are using their own right to free speech. A better way to make a joke is to make rapists or rape culture itself seem ridiculous rather than make fun of victims.

SCARED OF THE WORD, NOT THE ACTION

"[A]s long as the word 'rapist' didn't appear in the questionnaire, men were comfortable answering 'yes' to questions such as: 'Have you ever had sexual intercourse with an adult when they didn't want to because you used or threatened to use physical force?' In interviews ... it turned out that respondents somehow didn't realize that this was a description of rape."

—Sandra Newman, author

Sandra Newman, "Why Men Rape," Aeon, March 30, 2017. aeon.co/essays/until-we-treat-rapists-as-ordinary-criminals-we-wont-stop-them.

Catcalling and Groping

Catcalling is when men shout at women as they pass by on the street, and it is a form of sexual harassment. "Hey, baby," "Can I get a smile?," and "What's your number?" are all things women often hear when they walk down a sidewalk minding their own business, regardless of what they are wearing or what they look like. Men commonly dismiss women's fears about catcalling by insisting that it is a compliment—"Why can't you take a compliment?" is a common complaint heard when a woman rejects a catcaller—but most women would say they feel anything but complimented when a stranger calls out to them on the street. Generally, a compliment is something that makes a person feel good about themselves; fear, anger, and embarrassment are not generally associated with being complimented, although they are with catcalling. Male comedian Elon James White exposed this lie when he created the hashtag #DudesGreetingDudes on Twitter: "These women don't get it. Y'all just want to say hi. What's wrong with hi?!?! So let's just leave them out completely … Because it's not about sex or nothing. We just wanna say hi."[24] The idea behind it is that while many heterosexual male catcallers pretend they are giving a simple compliment, they would never say the kinds of things to another man that they say to a woman. Other Twitter users joined in, using the hashtag to tweet parodies of things women often hear, such as, "Hey handsome. Why you wearing them short sleeve shirts if you didn't want me to comment on your arms?"[25]

Catcalling can be frightening, especially for women walking alone.

Catcalling is an extension of rape culture because it carries the threat of sexual violence. Natalie Cortes of the National Organization for Women (NOW) explained the social interaction that goes on when a woman is catcalled:

> In the context of gender, harassment often ends up being a way for men to exert control over women and their bodies. Shouting a crude comment about a woman's appearance suggests entitlement to her body. Groping or stalking or simply standing too close without a woman's permission shows entitlement to her space. Expecting a woman to talk to you while or after you harass her displays entitlement to her time.[26]

When a man shouts at a woman on the street, he is making it clear to her that he is in charge. Theoretically, he could do whatever he wanted to her, and given the way society mishandles sexual assault and violence against women in general, he might get away with it.

Groping, or touching someone without their permission, is also a problem. In crowded places, it is easy for someone to touch another person in a private place, such as their backside or between their legs. In some places, such as Japan, groping is such an issue on public transportation that some train cars are designated women-only at peak travel times, such as the commute to and from work. Other countries have considered adopting this strategy, but opponents say it normalizes sexual assault and that women should not have to be separated from men to feel safe.

Slut-Shaming

"Slut-shaming is the experience of being labeled a sexually out-of-control girl or woman (a 'slut' or 'ho')," wrote Leora Tanenbaum of the *Huffington Post*, "and then being punished socially for possessing this identity. Slut-shaming is sexist because only girls and women are called to task for their sexuality, whether real or imagined; boys and men are congratulated for the exact same behavior."[27] Because of the cultural obsession with female purity and virginity, women who enjoy sex and may have had sex with multiple partners are often considered bad. They are also considered to be at fault if they are sexually assaulted, and the usual excuses (e.g. "Look at what she was wearing") are magnified when a woman has a sexual past. Even women who previously had no such reputation may be labeled "sluts" after being raped because people assume they must have been acting "slutty" for someone to want to rape them. However, again, sexual assault in all its forms is hardly ever only about sex; instead, it is about gaining power over the victim, so how a woman looks or acts has very little to do with her chances of being attacked. One example people use to prove this is that even women who are fully covered, such as Muslim women wearing burqas or other full-body coverings, have been raped. Additionally, just because a woman consents to have sex with a particular person does not mean she consents to have sex with everyone. For instance, if a woman goes to a bar hoping to find someone to have sex with later that night, she is still allowed to choose which person that will be, and she is allowed to refuse sexual advances from someone she is uninterested in.

A woman's clothing is simply an excuse; even women who are fully covered could potentially be raped.

Although many girls are banding together to fight slut-shaming, some still believe that sexually liberated women deserve it. People who disagree with slut-shaming often point the finger at these girls, wondering why they encourage hating other girls for their personal choices when they should be on the same side of the issue. The fact is that women who put other women down are suffering from internalized misogyny. Misogyny is the technical term for prejudice and hate against women, and it is one of the underlying reasons that rape culture continues. When women hear anti-woman statements all the time, some of them begin to believe them and try to force them onto other women. They want to be seen as "good" examples of women and distance themselves from the "bad" ones by shaming them, even though enjoying sex or being sexually assaulted are not things that make a woman bad.

Facing The Consequences

The consequences of rape culture are far-reaching, and each one serves to perpetuate rape culture further. The reason it is so difficult to find a solution to rape culture is because every problem stems from something so ingrained in people's minds that it will take generations to shift the way most of the population thinks. The cultural expectations people teach children often set them up as victims or abusers in later life, making it important that society understand how rape culture affects the way people interact both with kids and adults. They also cannot ignore the trauma caused by sexual assault and the way it hurts people long after they have been attacked.

Learning Fear

One of the main effects of rape culture is that women are taught to be afraid of everything, especially men. Parents always fear for their children's safety and want to protect them from danger, but the main danger for their daughters, unlike for their sons, is sexual violence. When raising girls, parents often feel the need to prepare them for living a life ruled by rape culture, where sexual assault is an inevitability. With one out of every six women being the survivor of a sexual assault, many mothers are survivors, making them even more fearful for their daughters' safety. To combat these fears, mothers pass them on by having conversations with their daughters about "not making themselves look like a victim," or about not walking by themselves at night, or about what to do if they think a man is following them. Unfortunately, these conversations generally focus on fearing strangers and leave out critical information about what to do if someone they know is sexually abusing them. Also, even though taking precautions for safety is a good idea, talking to daughters about protecting themselves and not having similar conversations with sons perpetuates two myths: that women are responsible for not being sexually assaulted and that men do not have to worry about being sexually assaulted.

Men also teach their daughters to be afraid of men. Some fathers make their daughters' dating lives their personal business rather than allowing them to make their own decisions, and this is "hurtful, offensive, and damaging,"[28] as Christine Organ put it in her article, "The Problem with the Overprotective Dad Stereotype." Not only does it teach girls that they need a man to protect them, it also teaches them that boys are naturally out of control and need to be protected against. Organ said, "Our boys deserve to be held to a higher standard than that,"[29] meaning that by assuming all boys are only after sex, society makes it socially acceptable for them to behave that way and creates prejudice against the ones who are not. This creates a loop, giving girls a reason to fear boys and feeding into rape culture.

Even though parents generally have their daughters' best interests at heart, some of their advice and warnings can hurt them in the future.

TALKING ABOUT SAFETY

"[Studies] found that when teaching their 2- and 4-year-old children to climb down a pole on a playground, mothers and fathers ... provided explanations to daughters three times more often, suggesting that parents thought girls needed more guidance about how to perform the activity than did boys. These studies suggest that parent–child conversations about safety may differ depending on the gender of the child."

—Elizabeth E. O'Neal, Jodie M. Plumert, and Carole Peterson, researchers

Elizabeth E. O'Neal, Jodie M. Plumert, and Carole Peterson, "Parent-Child Injury Prevention Conversations Following a Trip to the Emergency Department," *Journal of Pediatric Psychology*, vol. 41, no. 2 (March 1, 2016): p. 258. academic.oup.com/jpepsy/article/41/2/256/2579803/Parent-Child-Injury-Prevention-Conversations.

Keeping Girls in the Dark

In a society where young women are told that their sexuality is a shameful thing and where it is often used against them as proof that they deserve to be assaulted, many girls go uneducated about sex and sexuality in general. This leaves them vulnerable both emotionally and physically once they become sexually active.

There are several different kinds of sexual education classes: abstinence-only, abstinence-plus, and comprehensive. Abstinence-only classes teach that waiting until marriage is the only correct way to have sex; many use tactics that create fear and guilt, such as comparing girls who sleep with multiple men to used and dirty pieces of tape. Abstinence-plus classes teach students about the different kinds of protection, such as condoms and birth control pills, but stress that waiting until marriage is the best choice. Comprehensive sex education classes not only teach about protection, they also cover the emotional side, discussing things such as how to ask for and give consent, how to discuss problems in a relationship, and how to make sure both partners are enjoying the experience. Comprehensive sex education classes have been shown in multiple studies to have the most success in lowering both the teen pregnancy and abortion rates, but they are rare compared to abstinence-only and abstinence-plus classes.

Being uninformed about sex can make the experience confusing and even scary.

Abstinence-only and abstinence-plus classes in schools often gloss over the emotional side of sex, and very rarely do they teach about female pleasure. Both of these things are considered secondary when teaching young adults about sex, with sex education focusing more on the biological functions of sexual intercourse and on the male sexual response rather than the female. From these types of classes, girls learn that sex is not about them. In a presentation for TEDWomen in 2016, journalist and author Peggy Orenstein illustrated the negative impact of keeping young women uneducated about their wants and needs by comparing American girls to Dutch girls. She said:

> *Consider a survey of 300 randomly chosen girls from a Dutch and an American university, two similar universities, talking about their early experience of sex. The Dutch girls embodied everything we say we want from our girls. They had fewer negative consequences, like disease, pregnancy, regret—more positive outcomes*

Dress Codes

Colleges are known for perpetuating rape culture by mishandling accusations, but schools in general also promote rape culture by punishing girls for their clothing. Often school dress codes do not allow girls to wear clothes that show their shoulders or their backs, as well as not allowing shorts or skirts that go above the mid-thigh. Leggings and yoga pants have also made some banned clothing lists. Girls report being pulled aside and told to change by teachers and administrators, and some have even been given detention or suspended for wearing something deemed inappropriate. Boys, however, are not held to the same standards, and when boys physically or verbally harass girls in school, the girls are told, "He likes you," or "Boys will be boys." This creates an unhealthy association of violence with attraction; it also does not hold the boys accountable for their actions. According to Laura Bates, founder of the Everyday Sexism Project,

> When a girl is taken out of class on a hot day for wearing a strappy top, because she is "distracting" her male classmates, his education is prioritized over hers. When a school takes the decision to police female students' bodies while turning a blind eye to boys' behavior, it sets up a lifelong assumption that sexual violence is inevitable and victims are partially responsible.[1]

As part of a protest against the dress code at her middle school, sixth grader Molly Neuner wrote "#IAmNotADistraction" on her arm.

1. Laura Bates, "How School Dress Codes Shame Girls and Perpetuate Rape Culture," *TIME*, May 22, 2015. time.com/3892965/everydaysexism-school-dress-codes-rape-culture/

like being able to communicate with their partner, who they said they knew very well; preparing for the experience responsibly; enjoying themselves. What was their secret? The Dutch girls said that their doctors, teachers and parents talked to them candidly, from an early age, about sex, pleasure and the importance of mutual trust. What's more, while American parents weren't necessarily less comfortable talking about sex, we tend to frame those conversations entirely in terms or risk and danger, whereas Dutch parents talk about balancing responsibility and joy.[30]

Because rape culture focuses so heavily on the part the victim plays in their own assault, girls are taught to suppress their sexuality in the hope that it will keep them safe. At the same time, keeping them unaware about how sex should feel—many American girls believe sex is supposed to hurt, which has been proven false by medical experts—and about how they should be treated by their partners makes them less likely to recognize sexual abuse when it is happening.

Aggression and Violence

The patriarchy teaches young children that certain traits are naturally masculine or feminine, but social scientists say that many of the actions people associate with the binary genders are "performative," meaning people create gender based on what they do, not the other way around. Nevertheless, boys are under a great deal of pressure to perform masculinity even if it does not come naturally. Being seen as "girly" sometimes brings bullying from other boys who act more masculine and are therefore more socially accepted, and sometimes even parents can be harsh when their son does not live up to their expectations. All this pressure can lead to a phenomenon known as toxic masculinity, when masculine traits are taken to their extremes and are strictly enforced. There is nothing natural about it. As Ryan Douglass wrote on the *Huffington Post* website, "Toxic masculinity is built on two fundamental pillars: sexual conquest and violence—qualities men regale [praise] as manly and virtuous."[31] These two traits come together specifically under rape culture, which promotes sexual violence as the norm and supports toxic masculinity. If sexual violence is normal, then toxic masculinity is normal, and if toxic masculinity is normal, then sexual violence is normal. The two ideas feed each other.

The normalization of sexual violence opens the door for violence of all kinds to be normalized. The World Health Organization (WHO) estimates that worldwide, one-third of all women who have ever been in a relationship have experienced abuse at the hands of their partner, including "physical aggression, sexual coercion, psychological abuse and controlling behaviours,"[32] and one-third of all women on the planet have experienced physical or sexual violence in general. When it comes to toxic masculinity, physical violence is often the most talked about because aggression is so highly praised in men, and it is generally used as a display of dominance against marginalized groups. Women, different racial or ethnic groups, and LGBT+ people are often the targets of male violence.

When male stereotypes are too strongly enforced, men are likely to resort to violence when their power is threatened.

Child Abuse

Although people do not like to think about it, rape culture trickles down to children as well, and not just in the way gender is taught to them. Under the age of 18, 1 out of 9 girls and 1 out of 53 boys experience sexual assault. According to RAINN, 66 percent of them are 12 to 17 years old, and 34 percent of them are under 12. About 80 percent of the time, a parent is responsible for the abuse, with the other 20 percent made up of other adult relatives, siblings, friends of the family, strangers, and unmarried partners of a parent. Teenage girls, who are four times more likely to be sexually assaulted than the general population and cannot legally consent to sex no matter how mature they seem, are held to the same disturbing standards as adult women. They are often blamed for leading men on or for tricking men into sleeping with them because they looked mature. Although Child Protective Services (CPS) is generally better than the average police force at finding evidence of sexual abuse, society does little more for child victims than it does for adults.

For children, rape culture begins when adults refuse to respect their boundaries. Children are often expected to hug or kiss relatives even when they do not want to, and this tells them that their personal comfort zone is of less importance than the happiness of others. Being taught to respect authority without question, such as when a parent tells them do something "because I said so," does something similar, taking away their independence and forcing them to follow orders without understanding why they are doing it. These ideas make it difficult, if not impossible, for kids to say "no" to adults, making it easier for sexual abusers to get away with hurting them. Children also pick up on their parents' attitudes about things very early on, and because so many people refuse to educate their children about sex, children assume it is a bad thing and believe they will be in trouble if they tell someone they are being sexually abused. These problems often persist into adulthood, creating adults who cannot say "no" and feel so ashamed by sexual assault that they do not go to the authorities. By this time, however, distorted ideas about boundaries and authority are so deeply ingrained that adults believe they are normal and pass them on to their children.

Children know when they are uncomfortable even if they do not know how to put it into words, so guilting them into situations they are uncomfortable with can make them unable to trust their own instincts.

Effects of Trauma

A side effect of rape culture is the trauma rape survivors go through and the long-lasting mental and emotional scars. Physical trauma from a violent assault can include bruising, bleeding, and broken or dislocated bones. Sexually transmitted diseases (STDs) and pregnancy can also become health concerns. Getting an STD or becoming pregnant after an assault can prolong the physical healing time as well as cause additional emotional pain.

Even if sexual abuse does not leave physical marks, it almost always leaves marks on the brain. According to the Joyful Heart Foundation, a nonprofit organization that helps sexual assault survivors, 94 percent of rape survivors report having symptoms of PTSD for 2 weeks after being attacked, and 30 percent of those survivors report those same symptoms 9 months later. These symptoms include "flashbacks, nightmares, severe anxiety, and uncontrollable thoughts."[33] Dissociation, which involves being unable to focus and not feeling present in one's body on a regular or constant basis, is also commonly reported.

Dissociation can make it feel as though the body and mind are separate, making reality seem surreal and far away.

Triggers

In some cases of trauma, a person may become vulnerable to triggers, which are "any certain something [that] causes a negative emotional response."[1] They are generally things that remind the person of the traumatic event, but they can be literally anything—from a smell or a sound to a topic or idea. Gillian Brown, a writer for the website The Body Is Not An Apology, described being triggered as an "all-encompassing panic."[2] Sometimes, people are triggered by absolutely nothing, but that does not make their experience any less valid.

Similar to the way people will use the word "depression" to mean mild sadness rather than the serious mental disorder it is, the word "triggered" gets used a lot in ways that make it seem silly or unimportant. Many people, especially on the Internet, use it to belittle people who have different views than them. These same people attack survivors of trauma for becoming upset when they get triggered by something or for asking others to put content warnings in their hashtags. People who have never experienced trauma claim that trauma survivors should just "get over it," and that the world is not going to cater to them just because they might get triggered. What they do not understand, however, is that survivors cannot just "get over it," and most understand that the world is not sugarcoated. People who mock others for using trigger warnings imagine that being triggered simply means experiencing the normal human emotion of feeling unhappy when being reminded of an unpleasant event. In reality, a trigger can cause someone intense emotional pain, including depression, panic attacks, and thoughts of or attempts at suicide. Regardless, asking for one's Internet space to be safe is not unreasonable, and in some cases, it may be lifesaving.

1. Gillian Brown, "5 Ways to Help Your Friend if They Have Been Triggered," The Body Is Not An Apology, August 5, 2017, thebodyisnotanapology.com/magazine/the-beginners-guide-to-triggering/
2. Brown, "5 Ways to Help Your Friend."

Depression is also a common effect of sexual violence. Rape victims are about three times more likely to have a major depressive episode than the average person. Symptoms of depression include "prolonged sadness, feelings of hopelessness, unexplained crying, weight loss or gain, loss of energy or interest in activities previously enjoyed."[34] About 33 percent of women who have been sexually assaulted think about committing suicide, and about 13 percent actually attempt it. The rate of drug use is also very high among rape survivors; they are 3.4 times more likely to use marijuana, 6 times more likely to use cocaine, and 10 times more likely to use other hard drugs than the average person.

Emotions following a sexual assault can be hard to control and hard to deal with. Many survivors feel continuing fear, vulnerability, helplessness, anger, and self-blame, as well as shock and emotional numbness. These emotions can sometimes make a victim feel weak even though most of them are natural reactions to traumatic experiences. Some survivors also find that they have a hard time trusting people, even family and friends, and it seems that the closer the relationship to the abuser, the more likely issues with trust will affect personal and professional relationships.

What Can Be Done?

An article called "Ten Things to End Rape Culture" that was published in the *Nation* begins, "Rape culture exists because we don't believe it does."[35] Fighting something that so many people deny the existence of can be frustrating, but that does not mean it is hopeless. Change does not happen quickly, but it will not happen at all if people do nothing.

Although the future of rape culture remains unclear in the current political and social climate, everyone can do their part to prevent it in their homes, where they work and go to school, and in their communities. If more people made an individual effort to stop rape culture in their local area, the collective effect would transform society on a much larger scale.

Do Not Participate

One of the most important steps in ending rape culture is trying not to perpetuate it further, and not participating in activities that help it continue is the best way to keep it from spreading. Refusing to victim-blame or slut-shame when other people are doing it not only makes one less person contributing to the problem, but it sends a message to those other people that what they are doing is not okay. Like bullying, rape culture loses a lot of its power when people do not take part in it.

Another way to avoid participating in rape culture is to not consume products or entertainment media that glorify or make fun of sexual assault. In some ways, where people spend their money speaks the loudest. For years, advertising agencies have worked under the motto that "sex sells," but this often leads to the objectification of women, one of the main ways that Western culture tells people men are entitled to women's bodies. If a brand is famous for its oversexualized commercials, not buying their products or using their services takes away support for those kinds of advertising campaigns. In a similar way, some TV shows, movies, books, and music use objectification to sell themselves, and others handle the topic of sexual assault inappropriately. Committing to keeping money out of the pockets of people who are contributing to rape culture can be an effective form of protest known as boycotting. Learning about what to look for in media and advertising—such as oversexualized women, storylines that shame victims, and anything that glamorizes abusive relationships—is key to boycotting and making a difference.

This movie poster is an old example of oversexualized women in advertising, but modern ads are just as likely to use women's bodies to sell products.

The Bechdel Test and More

Created in 1985 by cartoonist Alison Bechdel and popularized in the early 2000s, the Bechdel Test is a series of criteria applied to movies and television shows to see if they have realistic female characters in them. To pass, they must have: (1) two named, female characters, (2) who have a conversation together, (3) that is not about a man. Although these rules seem simple, many pieces of media fail the Bechdel Test, although the test itself is not perfect and is not a true measure of how feminist a work is, since a number of films and television shows pass the test but still contain sexist material. However, it is a good starting place when thinking critically about media since it can be applied to film, television, and literature. Other similar tests include:

- the Mako Mori Test: "Named after a 'Pacific Rim' character … [t]he rules of the test are that the movie must have at least one female character, that character must get her own narrative arc, and the arc cannot be about a man's story."[1]

- the Sexy Lamp Test: "While watching the movie, think to yourself, 'is this woman important to the plot, or could she easily be removed or replaced?' If she can be replaced by a sexy lamp then that movie has officially failed the test."[2]

- the Furiosa Test: "Named after Imperator Furiosa from 'Mad Max: Fury Road,' the test demands a movie do one thing and one thing alone: make men upset … If the movie has men's rights activists moaning about 'women taking over' or 'ruining everything' or 'political correctness winning over good writing' when none of these things are true, then this is a movie you might wanna see over and over again."[3]

1. Christina Waters, "Feminist Tests to Judge Your Movies By," Odyssey Online, August 1, 2016, www.theodysseyonline.com/feminist-tests-judge-movies.
2. Waters, "Feminist Tests."
3. Waters, "Feminist Tests."

Speak Up

Speaking out against rape culture is another way to help change things. "Rape culture thrives in passive acceptance of female degradation, victim-blaming and hyper-masculinity in our communities, both physical and digital," said the *Nation*. "Report abuse on Facebook. Lobby college administrators for more safe spaces to discuss sexual assault on campus."[36] Making a ruckus keeps the conversation alive and does not allow people to brush the issues under the rug. Men need to join the conversation, too. Not only will that send the message to other men that rape culture is not an issue only women, transgender, and nonbinary people should care about, but it will also help make male victims more visible to the public.

The Internet gives people so many platforms that can be used to discuss and educate. Writing a blog post or making a video about an aspect of rape culture someone has personally observed or experienced can help broaden the amount of information out there about the topic, as well as bring the community together. It can also bring out trolls and start heated debates, so people who do this should make sure they are ready to engage with people reasonably if they are going to open the conversation. They also have the right to block and report someone who is harassing them or someone else online. Abusers should not get away with hurting people just because the abuse is taking place online. It is also important to remember that everyone has a different amount of knowledge about social issues, so if someone says something ignorant but does not mean to offend people by it, being lenient with them and taking the opportunity to educate them will work much better at changing their behavior than insulting them. Gently explaining what is wrong with someone's statement goes a lot farther than starting an argument.

Many of the same ideas apply in person. Trying to gather a community together to talk about sexual assault can be a great way of educating people and supporting survivors. It also helps for a person to speak up when someone they are having a conversation with is saying something problematic—for instance, if they start talking about how a girl deserved to be raped because of what she was wearing. As long as the person feels safe doing so in that moment, putting names to the real problems, such as toxic masculinity and victim-blaming, puts the spotlight on them rather than outdated ways of thinking.

Also, if someone becomes a victim of sexual assault or harassment, they should not be afraid to report it. Even though law enforcement sometimes mishandles sexual assault, it is better to report it and give justice a chance to be served than to stay silent. Nothing gets better when people stay silent.

Joining an online community can help relieve some of the effects of trauma, such as depression and distrust, by allowing survivors to share their thoughts and feelings with people who understand.

Make Space

Creating safe spaces for sexual assault survivors to talk about their experiences is not only vital for victims' mental and emotional health, but it can also be a way for the public to hear more individual stories and reevaluate their ideas about who victims are. Stereotypes about rape victims—that they are "sluts," that they brought it on themselves, that they are all women—help keep rape culture alive in people's minds, but all these stereotypes fall apart when actually faced with the variety of survivors and their stories.

Talking about trauma is one of the best ways to begin healing from it. Tovah Means, a psychotherapist, explained the conflicting emotions some sexual assault victims feel about reaching out for help: "This kind of trauma often leaves the survivor very confused about relationships ... It creates a dilemma where intimate relationships become terrifying and yet, as humans, we long for closeness and connection."[37] Many of the mental and emotional issues that linger after an assault do so because the survivor feels alone or guilty because rape culture isolates and blames them, but even talking to a friend or therapist privately can help relieve that emotional weight. Finding support is the top priority for the mental health of rape survivors, but many do not know where to start. Allies and fellow survivors need to make it known that they are there to listen and provide the support that is so desperately required.

Redefining Gender

As society moves into the future, the way people think about themselves and others is going to have to change if they want to end rape culture. A huge sticking point for older generations is gender, which has been traditionally defined as "male" or "female" and dictated by biological sex. This definition, however, is changing as both science and society have begun to question and challenge what sex and gender mean. Millennials and centennials, the two generations born after the 1970s, are the most liberated generations in terms of their rejection of traditional gender roles and their acceptance of people outside the gender binary.

Gender equality can only happen when people break down the division between masculine and feminine qualities.

One of the most important steps in stopping rape culture is redefining masculinity so it does not reach its extreme, toxic boiling point. This is one of the many goals of feminism, a social movement based in women's rights and fighting for equality for everyone. Feminists believe that by allowing men to have "feminine" qualities such as emotional vulnerability and the option to be dependent on their partners, the amount of toxic masculinity in Western culture can be decreased, therefore decreasing the amount of sexual assault that comes with it. Additionally, when "feminine" traits are no longer considered naturally weaker and inferior to "masculine" ones, women and other feminine people will be more equal in general, making the power imbalance that allows rape to go unreported smaller.

Teaching Consent

Another important change that needs to be made in society is how people educate children about consent. As it stands now, many kids grow up believing that their personal boundaries do not matter, which teaches them that the personal boundaries of others do not matter either. To combat this, children as young as one year old should be taught some basics about respecting personal space and should have their personal space respected in turn. Teaching kids to ask permission before touching someone, teaching them to listen when people say "stop" or "no," allowing them to make decisions and trust their instincts, and teaching them to use their words to communicate rather than throwing temper tantrums are all good ways for parents to make sure their children understand boundaries and how to assert themselves.

Rape culture thrives on a "'no' means 'yes'" attitude, a popular sentiment found in misogynist groups, and the idea that simply because someone does not say "no" means they have said "yes." The biggest threat to rape culture is learning about consent and putting it into practice. The *Nation* stated that although rape culture makes people likely to try to find excuses for rapists,

> *Enthusiastic consent—the idea that we're all responsible to make sure that our partners are actively into whatever's going down*

"Feminist" Is Not a Bad Word

With feminism on the rise among young people, others who disagree with the idea have begun a campaign against it, making fun of people who call themselves feminists and spreading false information about feminism's philosophies to scare curious people away. In the simplest terms, being a feminist means someone advocates for women's rights, but some believe that means they hate men, which the vast majority of feminists do not. In fact, feminism fights for men's rights as well by questioning gender roles and attempting to free men, along with women, from the restrictions of the patriarchy; a commonly quoted phrase among feminists is "The patriarchy hurts everyone." In addition to this, feminism has evolved over the years from its roots in the women's suffrage movement, and today it includes people of color and LGBT+ people in its fight for equality. This is called intersectional feminism—recognizing that people with different traits experience oppression in different ways. For instance, white women generally make less money than men do for the same work, and black women make even less than white women.

Throughout the early 1900s, suffragettes fought for the American woman's right to vote, the first step toward gender equality in the United States. Today, feminists continue to fight for equality.

between us sexually—takes a lot of those excuses away. Rather than looking for a 'no,' make sure there's an active 'yes.' If you adopt enthusiastic consent yourself, and then teach it to those around you, it can soon become a community value.[38]

The key word here is "enthusiastic." The only time someone should go ahead with any sexual activity is after hearing a definite "yes"—not just agreement, but eager agreement.

Some communities have created consent public service announcements (PSAs), which are short videos that air on the radio or TV during commercial breaks. PSAs educate people about important topics, such as alcohol and drug abuse, domestic abuse, and sexual violence. In one Scottish PSA, two men at a bar watch a woman talk and laugh with a different group of men. One of the watching men says to his friend, "Check out her skirt. She is asking for it."[39] The scene immediately switches to the woman in a department store, trying to choose between two skirts. When a saleswoman asks if she can help, the woman says, "Yeah, thanks. I'm going out tonight and I want to get raped. I need a skirt that will encourage a guy to have sex with me against my will."[40] This statement shows how ridiculous it is to think that someone would be "asking for it." The PSA ends with the words, "Nobody asks to be raped. Ever."[41]

SUPPORT FOR CONSENT EDUCATION

"New data on consent and sexual assault make it crystal clear that more needs to be done to educate men, women, and young people in this country. Most people have not received any education about what consent is, what it looks like, or how to do it. It's no wonder there is still disagreement and confusion."

—Dr. Leslie Kantor, vice president of education at Planned Parenthood Federation of America

Quoted in "New Study: Overwhelming Support for Consent Education in Schools," Planned Parenthood Action Fund, April 21, 2016. www.plannedparenthoodaction.org/blog/overwhelming-support-for-consent-education-in-schools.

Anti-rape campaigns generally focus on the need for consent because it is the easiest and quickest way to reduce sexual assault.

National and Global Strategies

On a national level in the United States, the Violence Against Women Act (VAWA) protects survivors of domestic abuse and sexual assault, and it is not only limited to women. Everyone in the United States benefits from the services the act provides. "Initially passed in 1994, VAWA created the first U.S. federal legislation acknowledging domestic violence and sexual assault as crimes, and provided federal resources to encourage community-coordinated responses to combating violence,"[42] according to the National Network to End Domestic Violence. Ultimately, the act increased the number of reports of abuse and assault by 51 percent for women and 37 percent for men, and it saved the country at least $12.6 billion over the first six years after it was signed into law. It also created the Rape Prevention and Education (RPE) program at the Centers for Disease Control and Prevention (CDC). This program helps educate communities about rape and sexual assault and provides funding to state health departments to enhance their rape prevention measures.

Globally, the Convention on the Elimination of All Forms of Discrimination against Women and the UN Declaration on the Elimination of Violence against Women protect women in countries all over the world. The United Nations (UN), an organization that brings countries together to solve worldwide problems, adopted these agreements in 1979 and 1994, respectively, to ensure the safety of women in the UN member countries. UN Women, a UN organization dedicated to gender equality, has made it its mission to end violence, including sexual violence, against women all over the world.

Making the world a safer place for women and other marginalized groups is not easy. Systems that rely on inequality and prejudice make it difficult to convince those in power that they should care about people less fortunate than them. Violence is always a way to display dominance, and sexual violence is no exception. With education and understanding, however, it is possible that rape culture will fade into history like so many other outdated beliefs.

It is up to state and local health departments to make sure the public is well-informed about sexual health, including rape and consent.

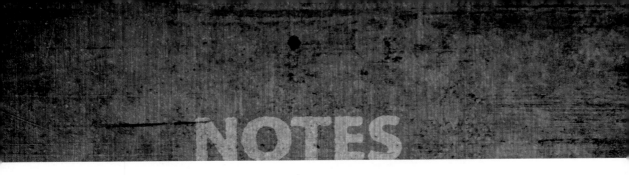

Introduction: A Serious Violation

1. Quoted in Natasha Tracy, "Young Girl Raped by 'Friend' and Called a Whore," Healthy Place, last modified February 10, 2016. www.healthyplace.com/abuse/rape/young-girl-raped-by-friend-and-called-a-whore/.

2. Susan B. Carbon, "An Updated Definition of Rape," United States Department of Justice, January 6, 2012. www.justice.gov/archives/opa/blog/updated-definition-rape.

3. "Sexual Harassment," U.S. Equal Employment Opportunity Commission, accessed June 26, 2017. www.eeoc.gov/laws/types/sexual_harassment.cfm.

Chapter 1: Cultural Roots

4. Nghiem L. Nguyen, "Roman Rape: An Overview of Roman Rape Laws from the Republican Period to Justinian's Reign," *Michigan Journal of Gender and Law*, vol. 13, no. 1 (2006): pp. 76–77, accessed June 1, 2017. repository.law.umich.edu/mjgl/vol13/iss1/3.

5. Nguyen, "Roman Rape," p. 84.

6. Joshua J. Mark, "Mythology," *Ancient History Encyclopedia*, last modified September 2, 2009. www.ancient.eu/mythology/.

7. Deuteronomy 22:28-29 (Revised Standard Version).

8. Donna Zuckerberg, "He Said, She Said: The Mythical History of the False Rape Allegation," *Jezebel*, July 30, 2015. jezebel.com/he-said-she-said-the-mythical-history-of-the-false-ra-1720945752.

9. Sean McGlynn, "Violence and the Law in Medieval England," *History Today*, vol. 58, no. 4 (April 2008), accessed July 11, 2017. www.historytoday.com/sean-mcglynn/violence-and-law-medieval-england.

10. McGlynn, "Violence and the Law in Medieval England."

11. Vaijayanti Joshi, "Female Hysteria During Victorian Era: Its Symptoms, Diagnosis & Treatment/Cures," Victorian-Era, accessed September 15, 2017. www.victorian-era.org/female-hysteria-during-victorian-era.html.

Chapter 2: Modern Problems

12. "Male Victims," National Alliance to End Sexual Violence, accessed September 13, 2017. endsexualviolence.org/where-we-stand/male-victims.

13. Juliana Breines, "Why Do We Blame Victims?," *Psychology Today*, November 24, 2013. www.psychologytoday.com/blog/in-love-and-war/201311/why-do-we-blame-victims.

14. Sheryl Gay Stolberg and Jess Bidgood, "Some Women Won't 'Ever Again' Report a Rape in Baltimore," *New York Times*, August 11, 2016. www.nytimes.com/2016/08/12/us/baltimore-police-sexual-assault-gender-bias.html?mcubz=0.

15. "What to Expect from the Criminal Justice System," RAINN, accessed September 6, 2017. www.rainn.org/articles/what-expect-criminal-justice-system.

16. "Criminal and Civil Justice," National Center for Victims of Crime, accessed September 7, 2017. victimsofcrime.org/media/reporting-on-child-sexual-abuse/criminal-and-civil-justice.

17. "What to Expect from the Criminal Justice System," RAINN.

18. Nathan J. Robinson, "Getting Away with It," *Current Affairs*, January 26, 2017. www.currentaffairs.org/2017/01/getting-away-with-it.

19. Quoted in Andy Battaglia, "Will Emma Sulkowicz's Protest *Mattress* Wind Up in a Museum?," *Vulture*, May 28, 2015. www.vulture.com/2015/05/does-sulkowiczs-mattress-belong-in-a-museum.html.

20. Marina Koren, "Telling the Story of the Stanford Rape Case," *The Atlantic*, June 6, 2016. www.theatlantic.com/news/archive/2016/06/stanford-sexual-assault-letters/485837/.

21. Michele Dauber, Twitter post, June 4, 2016, 9:58 p.m. twitter.com/mldauber/status/739320585222660096.

Chapter 3: A Harmful Cycle

22. Quoted in Katie Madden, "Rape Culture: The Media's Role in Normalizing Assault," *Campus Times*, May 16, 2014. lvcampustimes.org/2014/05/rape-culture-the-medias-role-in-normalizing-assault/.

23. Lindy West, "How to Make a Rape Joke," *Jezebel*, July 12, 2012. jezebel.com/5925186/how-to-make-a-rape-joke.

24. Quoted in Alex McKinnon, "#DudesGreetingDudes Is the Anti-Catcalling Hashtag of Your Dreams," Junkee, November 6, 2014. junkee.com/dudesgreetingdudes-is-the-anti-catcalling-hashtag-of-your-dreams/44539.

25. Quoted in McKinnon, "#DudesGreetingDudes."

26. Natalie Cortes, "Catcalling Is Not a Compliment," National Organization for Women, June 18, 2015. now.org/blog/catcalling-is-not-a-compliment/.

27. Leora Tanenbaum, "The Truth About Slut-Shaming," *Huffington Post*, June 15, 2015. www.huffingtonpost.com/leora-tanenbaum/the-truth-about-slut-shaming_b_7054162.html.

Chapter 4: Facing the Consequences

28. Christine Organ, "The Problem with the Overprotective Dad Stereotype," *Scary Mommy*, accessed September 22, 2017. www.scarymommy.com/overprotective-dad-stereotype/.

29. Organ, "The Problem with the Overprotective Dad Stereotype."

30. Peggy Orenstein, "What Young Women Believe About Their Own Sexual Pleasure," presentation, TEDWomen, San Francisco, CA, October 26-28, 2016. www.ted.com/talks/peggy_orenstein_what_young_women_believe_about_their_own_sexual_pleasure.

31. Ryan Douglass, "More Men Should Learn the Difference Between Masculinity and Toxic Masculinity," *Huffington Post*, August 4, 2017. www.huffingtonpost.com/entry/the-difference-between-masculinity-and-toxic-masculinity_us_59842e3ce4b0f2c7d93f54ce.

32. "Violence Against Women," World Health Organization, updated November 2016. www.who.int/mediacentre/factsheets/fs239/en/.

33. "Effects of Sexual Assault and Rape," Joyful Heart Foundation, accessed September 23, 2017. www.joyfulheartfoundation.org/learn/sexual-assault-rape/effects-sexual-assault-and-rape.

34. "Effects of Sexual Assault and Rape," Joyful Heart Foundation.

Chapter 5: What Can Be Done?

35. Walter Moseley, "Ten Things to End Rape Culture," ed. Rae Gomes, *Nation*, February 4, 2013. www.thenation.com/article/ten-things-end-rape-culture/.

36. Moseley, "Ten Things to End Rape Culture."

37. Tovah Means, interview by the Breathe Network, "Creating Safe Spaces for Healing Sexual Violence: An Interview with Tovah Means," Breathe Network, accessed September 24, 2017. www.thebreathenetwork.org/creating-safe-spaces-for-healing-sexual-violence-an-interview-with-tovah-means.

38. Moseley, "Ten Things to End Rape Culture."

39. "Not Ever," YouTube video, 0:30, posted by Rape Crisis Scotland, June 30, 2010. www.youtube.com/watch?v=h95-IL3C-Z8.

40. "Not Ever," YouTube video, posted by Rape Crisis Scotland.

41. "Not Ever," YouTube video, posted by Rape Crisis Scotland.

42. "Violence Against Women Act," National Network to End Domestic Violence, accessed September 24, 2017. nnedv.org/policy/issues/vawa.html.

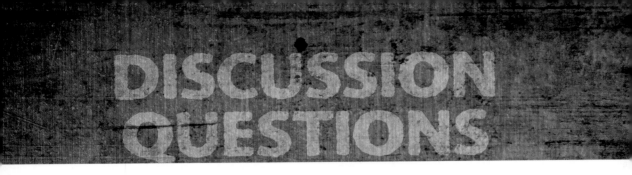

Chapter 1:
Cultural Roots

1. Are women still treated today the way they were in ancient times? Support your answer.

2. Were ancient laws regarding rape fair?

3. How do you feel about the gray area surrounding rape accusations?

Chapter 2:
Modern Problems

1. What are some more common examples of the "just world theory"?

2. What are some pros and cons of a civil court case versus a criminal court case?

3. Should colleges be in charge of sexual assault investigations on their own campuses?

Chapter 3:
A Harmful Cycle

1. What are some "masculine" and "feminine" traits? Are they positive or negative?

2. Should comedians be allowed to make rape jokes? Support your answer.

3. Do you see slut-shaming in your community? If so, what do you notice about it?

Chapter 4:
Facing the Consequences

1. Should fathers be overprotective of their daughters? Why or why not?

2. What might be some effects of toxic masculinity on society?

3. How might trauma after a sexual assault affect people other than the survivor?

Chapter 5:
What Can Be Done?

1. How does boycotting send a message about rape culture?

2. Why do you think younger people are so accepting of other people's differences?

3. What are some other ways people can stop rape culture in their communities?

4. What do you think the future of rape culture will look like?

Crisis Text Line

741741

www.crisistextline.org

> Texting HOME to this number automatically connects someone who is experiencing a crisis—which can be defined as any strongly painful emotion for which a person needs support, such as suicidal thoughts or a PTSD flashback—with a trained crisis counselor. This counselor will text with the person until they feel calmer. Counselors do not provide psychological or medical advice, only a listening ear and sympathetic responses.

Cultures of Consent

(202) 930-3744

www.culturesofconsent.org

info@culturesofconsent.org

> This nonprofit organization, which serves the northeastern United States, provides educational programs and information about consent. The website includes a resource library of articles covering sexual health and rape culture.

MaleSurvivor

PO Box 276

Long Valley, NJ 07853

www.malesurvivor.org

> This organization is committed to male sexual assault survivors. It provides resources and support for male victims.

National Alliance to End Sexual Violence

1129 20th Street NW, Suite 801
Washington, DC 20036
www.endsexualviolence.org
info@endsexualviolence.org

This national network of local rape crisis centers and state anti–sexual violence organizations analyzes and tracks government legislation, gives interviews, and advises Congress on the best ways for the government to support survivors.

Pandora's Project

3109 W. 50th Street, Suite 320
Minneapolis, MN 55410
www.pandys.org
admin@pandys.org

Pandora's Project is a nonprofit organization that provides resources and support for survivors of sexual assault and their families. The website offers a chat room and message board, a free lending library, and articles on reclaiming one's life after an assault.

Rape, Abuse, and Incest National Network (RAINN)

(202) 544-1034
hotline: (800) 656-4673
www.rainn.org

RAINN is the nation's largest anti–sexual violence organization. It operates the National Sexual Assault Hotline, provides statistics and information on rape and rape prevention, and organizes programs to help survivors find justice.

Take Back the Night Foundation

(888) 995-1113
www.takebackthenight.org

This volunteer charity foundation is focused on ending sexual violence and domestic abuse. It organizes marches and events to show solidarity against rape and assault, provides free legal assistance to survivors, and promotes survivor stories.

Books

Ghafoerkhan, Olivia. *Sexual Assault: The Ultimate Teen Guide.* Lanham, MD: Rowman & Littlefield, 2017.
> This book provides strategies and tools to help teenage readers deal with sexual assault and gives resources to help them find support.

Hiber, Amanda. *Sexual Violence.* Detroit, MI: Greenhaven Press, 2014.
> This book explores contrasting viewpoints on important questions about sexual violence, such as what causes it, how it should be addressed, and how it can be reduced.

Klein, Rebecca. *Rape and Sexual Assault.* New York, NY: Rosen Publishing, 2014.
> This guide to coping with sexual assault for survivors and friends of survivors provides detailed information about reporting assault and finding emotional support.

Marriott, Emma. *Violence Against Women.* New York, NY: Crabtree Publishing, 2017.
> The author examines acts of violence against women and girls all over the world, including human trafficking, murder, and domestic and sexual abuse.

Pardes, Bronwen. *Doing It Right: Making Smart, Safe, and Satisfying Choices About Sex.* New York, NY: Simon Pulse, 2013.
> This book informs young adults about sex-related issues such as anatomy, STDs, birth control, gender and sexual identity, sexual readiness, and rape.

Websites

End Rape on Campus (EROC)
www.endrapeoncampus.org
> This organization is dedicated to stopping campus sexual assault and providing college students with knowledge about their legal rights and how to get help from their school.

Futures Without Violence
www.futureswithoutviolence.org
> This organization is focused on ending violence against women and children around the world. It provides programs, campaigns, and online information about the issues of domestic and sexual violence.

Human Rights Campaign (HRC)
www.hrc.org
> This LGBT+ rights group has information about how rape culture affects the LGBT+ community and resources on getting specialized help and support.

Men Can Stop Rape
www.mencanstoprape.org
> This nonprofit organization gives information on how men can take responsibility for ending rape culture.

National Sexual Violence Resource Center (NSVRC)
www.nsvrc.org
> The NSVRC is a group that offers resources on preventing and responding to sexual assault, as well as promoting research into the topic of sexual violence.

Planned Parenthood
www.plannedparenthood.org
> This nonprofit health care provider and education center has information and resources about sexual health, including STDs, pregnancy, and sexual consent.

Scarleteen

www.scarleteen.com

For teens who feel that their sex education classes are not answering all their questions, Scarleteen has advice columns on topics such as birth control, sexual autonomy, creating a healthy relationship, issues that affect the LGBT+ community, and more. A live chat is available, and readers can submit their questions to the advice columnists.

INDEX

ABOUT THE AUTHOR

Michelle Denton received her bachelor's degree in English and creative writing from Canisius College in 2016, graduating cum laude from the All-College Honors Program. She lives in Buffalo, New York, with her mother and two cats and has made writing her full-time career. She also works as props master and sometimes-stage manager at the Subversive Theatre Collective, and she is currently trying to find the time to write her first novel.

2